*To my husband, Bob, who has supported
me through several launches.*

Kay

*To my wife, Elizabeth, who has always
helped launch my flights of fancy.*

Phil

Launching Leaders

Taking leadership development
to new heights

Kay L. Kotan
and
Phil Schroeder

Market
Square
BOOKS

Launching Leaders

Taking leadership development to new heights

©2019 Kay Kotan and Phil Schroeder

books@marketsquarebooks.com
P.O. Box 23664 Knoxville, Tennessee 37933

ISBN: 978-1-950899-03-6
Library of Congress: 2019943938

Printed and Bound in the United States of America
Cover Illustration & Book Design ©2019 Market Square Publishing, LLC
Publisher: Kevin Slimp
Editor: Kristin Lighter
Post-Process Editor: Ken Rochelle

Where noted, Scripture quotations are from:

(NRSV)
The New Revised Standard Version Bible, copyright © 1989 National
Council of the Churches of Christ in the United States of America.
Used by permission. All rights reserved worldwide.

(NIV)
THE HOLY BIBLE, NEW INTERNATIONAL VERSION®, NIV®
Copyright © 1973, 1978, 1984, 2011 by Biblica, Inc.® Used by permission.
All rights reserved worldwide.

(MSG)
Scripture quotations marked "MSG" or "The Message"
are taken from The Message. © 1993, 1994, 1995, 1996, 2000, 2001, 2002.
Used by permission of NavPress Publishing Group.

Table of Contents

Introduction

As congregational developers, it is one of the most requested resources: How do I identify, equip, and deploy leaders in my church? It seems as though we have a leadership crisis in the church. The crisis is not only in one lane. We struggle with leadership for both laity and clergy. Clergy are frustrated they cannot find enough leaders, or the leaders they do find are not mature in faith. Laity are frustrated that others are not stepping up into leadership, as well as sometimes their pastor does not exhibit maturity in his/her leadership skills. Denominational leaders are frustrated that leadership skills are missing in both clergy and laity. Denominational leaders look for the seminaries to develop leaders and the seminaries look to the denominational leadership structures to provide the leadership equipping.

The interesting situation is that while we have identified the problem – lack of leadership or leadership development – many have not yet addressed the situation with any solutions. We continue to moan and groan about the situation, but have taken no measurable action to remedy the situation. In our consulting with hundreds of congregations across the country, we could probably count on one or two hands the number of congregations who have an intentional leadership development process in place. There are even some annual conferences who lack this vital focus and equipping.

The Call for Leaders

Why is leadership so important? Why do we need solid leadership in the church? Why do we hunger so much for effective leadership? Competent leadership provides direction, accountability, guidance, and support. Leaders also provide motivation and direction toward a common purpose and goals. Leaders are cheerleaders for productivity, effectiveness, and efficiency. Good leaders are role models and mentors for developing leadership in others. Leaders strengthen the people and organization they are serving. Without leadership there is no forward momentum. The people and organization become stuck at best and often times decline. Leaders point and lead people towards the organization's vision. Leaders are equippers. Leaders not only manage change and conflict well, they are sometimes the ones that initiate it because it leads the organization in accomplishing its mission and vision.

Leadership is not a luxury. Mediocre leadership is not helpful and it sometimes hurtful. Great leaders are a necessity! If we are to become competent, compelling churches accomplishing our mission to make new disciples of Jesus Christ for the transformation of our communities and the world, we are simply going to need to have more great leaders leading the march to do so. Because we know few people are born as natural leaders, we must become intentional in having leadership expectations and providing training to become effective leaders. Leadership is not optional, it is essential.

In working on the book *Necessary Nine,* I (Kay) along with Bob Farr asked the question, "Are leaders born or developed?" We came to the conclusion that the answer is yes. Some are born with traits that have a tendency towards great leadership. Other leaders develop themselves as leaders. Yet, other leaders are poured into by other great leaders and have a willingness to learn and develop. You might say that some people decide to become a great leader and do all they need to resource themselves, find mentors, and dive deep into learning how to become a competent leader. While some might suggest if you are not a natural-born leader, you will never be a leader, we suggest that with a deep conviction to become a leader, most anyone can become a great leader. Leaders must consistently be a work in progress. They adapt, learn, grow, and stretch themselves consistently for continuous development.

In the The United Methodist Church, the *Book of Discipline* requires a Nominations and Lay Leadership Development Committee regardless of what type of structure the church uses. Most "Nominations Committees" do just that. They work through the nominations process to fill the needed committee vacancies for the upcoming year. Often the nominations process goes something like this: The committee gathers, the pictorial directory is pulled out, and the people who are not currently serving are identified. Then, the committee strategizes on who should call the identified suspect for the best chance at a positive response. When all the suspects have been gathered, the nominations committee has happily completed their work for the year. Sometimes the nominations committee is even touted as the easiest committee to work on since they only have to "work" a month or two a year.

We often struggle with leadership qualifications. Often with a lack of intentionality in the process of most nominations committees as described above, we are simply trying to get someone (or maybe anyone) to say "Yes" to filling the committee slot. In other churches, we are looking for people who have special training in secular jobs. We might be looking for someone with building experience for trustees, for financial experience for finance, or for human resources work experience for staff parish relations.

While these areas of experience and expertise can be helpful, without the expertise being undergirded in spiritual maturity, we are missing the boat. We are not seeing the bigger need. (Perhaps this is why we have ourselves in the current leadership crisis.) Our church leaders should be the most mature disciples of Jesus Christ. That is the most important trait we should be looking for in our leaders.

We can find those areas of expertise anywhere, but mature disciples are the ones that should be at the leadership table setting direction and leading the church into God's preferred future. Without mature disciples at the table, the church can be led into directions that are secularly driven rather than Holy Spirit driven. See more about this in Kotan's book, *Mission Possible*.[1]

We believe there is more! Actually, there is a requirement for more. The Nominations and Lay Leadership Development Committee is under the leadership of the pastor. This committee is not only responsible for the nomination of leaders to fulfill the required committee positions, but the committee is also responsible for lay leadership development. This leadership development responsibility is just as import-

---

1 Kotan, Kay and Bradford, Blake, *Mission Possible,* Market Square Books, 2019

4

ant as the nominations responsibility, if not more so, for this committee. Unfortunately, most nominations committees are unaware of these two distinct areas. However, when this committee does understand their role and acts upon these areas of responsibility, look out! What a huge difference this can make in the life of the congregation. Scripture also calls us to more in Deuteronomy 1:13, asking us to choose leaders who are wise, discerning, and reputable (NRSV). Or in Exodus 18:21 where Moses is instructed to look for people who fear God, are trustworthy, and hate dishonest gain.

Bottom line: We must have an intentional leadership development process in each and every church. We must identify potential leaders and invite them into the leadership process. We must journey alongside people in the leadership development process. We must help developed leaders find a meaningful place to serve in leadership that fits their gifts, skills, and passions. We must have a continual flow of people in and through the leadership development process.

Now that we have established the importance and need (or shall we say requirement) for a leadership development process, let's look at the leadership traits introduced in the first book of the Bible and one from the beginning of Mark.

Revealing Questions from Genesis and Mark

Where are you? Genesis 3:9

In this simple yet complex question, God asked a very profound question. This question causes one to ask the bigger question of vision, "Where are you and where are we going?" One cannot be a visionary if she/he is not a great communicator. Thus, the first trait of Christian leadership is to provide helpful communication. Without this foundational skill, there will be no underpinning to build the other leadership traits upon. The number one leadership trait is to be a helpful communicator with God and with others.

What are you to do with us? Mark 1:24

In other translations, this question is, "What business do you have with us?" While casting the vision in a compelling way is a must, we must also be able to engage in two-way conversations, too. We must be willing to listen as much as we are willing to speak. We often hear we are given one mouth and two ears for a reason. We need to listen twice as much as we speak. In addition to being able to be a helpful communicator, we must also be open to having worthwhile conversations that are meaningful, spiritual, life-giving, and provide forward momentum. The second leadership trait is to be in practice of holding holy conversations.

Why this tantrum/sulking? Genesis 4:6-7

We are often led to believe that a healthy church is a church with no conflict. However, if there is no conflict, the church is likely plateaued or may be in decline. When no conflict is present, the church is stuck and apathy might even be present. If the church is pushing the limits, living on the edge, and growing in its willingness and ability to reach new people for Christ, there will be conflict. No conflict means unhealthiness. No conflict usually means complacency has become the norm. Conflict is a good thing, a healthy thing. What is important is how we manage conflict. Healthy leaders embrace conflict. They even run towards conflict. A healthy amount of conflict is to be expected, but not ignored. The third leadership trait is healthy conflict.

Did you eat from the tree I told you not to eat from?
Genesis 3:11

This question causes us to be truth tellers and to be able to hear the truth from others. We call this leadership trait healing candor. I (Kay) often share with people (who I need to provide some uncomfortable observations with) that as a coach and consultant, I have a responsibility to provide the mirror of reflection in the situation so people can see their current reality through a delivery that I hope is full of love and grace. So, in other words, healing candor can be described as reconciling honesty. The fourth leadership trait is healing candor.

Who told you that you were naked? *Genesis 3:11*

In this next question, one's limitations are exposed. There is a submission that occurs. Yet, one has to believe in the vision and leading people into that vision. This question exposes us to a balanced leadership style we call "humbled confidence." One must exhibit the traits to lead that come from a place of self-confidence. With too much confidence, however, one can become arrogant. In that arrogance, one can become blind to their own shortcomings. The fifth leadership trait is to lead with humbled confidence.

Where is your brother? *Genesis 4:9*

In churches we often have the best of intentions. Frequently, we struggle to implement our ideas, or we call our work "good enough." We also sometimes

struggle with aligning our churches to the mission
of making disciples. In other words, we struggle with
accountability. We also sometimes struggle with
continuing to steep ourselves in our own stew over and
over again. We do not seek outside assistance or perspective. We often even lose sight of who our neighbors are and
how to reach them for Jesus Christ. We must continuously
seek collaborations that push us more and more into our
purpose, even if it is difficult. We must also provide direction that is both urgent and hope-filled for our congregations. The sixth leadership trait of a Christian leader is to
develop hope-filled collaborations.

What is it that you have done? Genesis 4:10

Great leaders are constantly growing. If a leader is not
continuously growing and learning, she/he will soon
become irrelevant and no longer be fully equipped to lead.
During my more than a decade of coaching leaders, I (Kay)
have found an inordinate number of church leaders who
lack self-awareness and, as a result, seem un-coachable.
Leaders must be willing to be fully self-aware of who
they are, who they aren't, and be willing to continuously
self-evaluate as they continuously grow and evolve as a
person, a follower of Christ, and a leader. I have run across
leaders who have come to the unfortunate conclusion
that they have all the answers and do not need or want
to be coached or even coaxed. The most effective leaders
work with a coach or coaches, both formal and informal,
to consistently evaluate, grow, and close the gap of where
they are and where God is calling them. The last leadership trait is being holistically coachable.

Today's world calls for leaders, as we have already established. We would challenge our readers to consider this: not only do we need to raise up new leaders, we need to raise up spiritual leaders. To take it even a step further, we don't just need to raise up spiritual leaders, we need to raise up gutsy, spiritual leaders. We would define gutsy spiritual leaders as people who are spiritually mature and are not afraid to risk for the sake of the Kingdom. You will not find this resource to be a safe play. No, quite the opposite. This resource pushes the envelope of the expectations of a traditional church leader. After all, we believe we have the crisis in spiritual leadership because we have been, indeed, playing it too safe. It is time to equip, release, and encourage gutsy spiritual leaders! God's Word calls for leaders and calls leaders.

In this resource, we will offer two sections. Section One offers an in-depth look at each of the gutsy leadership traits. Section Two offers the process of how to develop leaders. Section One offers the *what*. Section two offers the *how*. Since we have sufficiently covered the *why*, let's develop some gutsy spiritual leaders for Christ!

Part One

Orientation

As we begin to explore developing spiritual leadership, we need to unpack a couple of aspects of leadership development. First, in order to grow into anything new, we know we need begin to live outside our current reality, outside our comfort zone. Growth causes us to stretch beyond our current situation. In order to grow into something new and make it sustainable, we know it needs to become habitual. In order to become habitual, we know we must first offer to repeat our new way of being and/or doing with consistency. Therefore, to live into being the best leader possible, we must pursue being a great leader with habitual consistency. We must consistently live into forming and reforming ourselves with intentional new habits to continuously evolve into a better, gutsy spiritual leader every day.

Being a leader today takes some tenacity. Great spiritual leaders are what we refer to as gutsy leaders. Gutsy leaders take chances. Gutsy leaders experiment. Gutsy leaders are constant innovators. Trying new things is a must, even at the risk of failing. Gutsy leaders see failing as only the opportunity to have learned something new to apply to the next experiment. Gutsy leaders take calculated risks on new ventures. Gutsy leaders are consistently living at the edges of their own personal and professional comfort zone. I (Kay) once had someone tell me the reason they liked being around me is that I was always living life on the edge, and therefore didn't take up much room here on the planet. Complacency and apathy are not in the vocabulary of gutsy leaders.

Before you can lead others, you must first be able to lead yourself. Before you can lead a group of others, you must first learn to lead yourself, and then lead another. Too often we jump to trying to lead the world without first learning to lead ourselves. In Kotan & Farr's book *The Necessary Nine: Things Effective Pastors Do Differently,* the levels of leadership are identified on page 32:

Levels of Leadership

1. Self

2. Leading another

3. Leading a team

4. Leading an organization

5. Leading leaders

6. Leading a network

7. Leading the world.

Gutsy Leaders know how to fly, so in this resource we will be using a flying metaphor to describe how to "launch leaders." In order to learn how to fly, a pilot must first attend ground school. Think of Section One as attending ground school. Ground school is about learning, conditioning, and fundamentals. Part One can be read on its own and stand alone as a leadership resource. If working through the material as a group, consider reading a chapter in part one individually, then discussing it as a group, using the direction provided in Part 2. Section Two is the preflight checklist or flight checklist designed to be done with a group of people. Part Two is beginning to practice what is learned in ground school. Part Two prepares you to lead others. Part Two begins to build healthy leadership habits.

Besides Parts One and Two, you will find a Wrap Up section in this resource. Think of the Wrap Up section as the "taking flight" or being "launched" into the gutsy spiritual leadership portion of being your best you.

Power of Habits: Consistent Habits for Launched Leaders

We have already introduced the concept of a great spiritual leader having positive traits and developing healthy habits. Being spiritually grounded and having spiritual disciplines is at the heart of a good Christian leader. We believe the leadership traits we have identified can be reinforced by a spiritual habit or discipline, based on the work of Michael Foss in *Power Surge.*[2] Each chapter will unpack the trait and its corresponding habits. This will give you the opportunity to be simultaneously developing the corresponding leadership and spiritual habits in each step of the development journey.

Leadership Habits:	Spiritual Habits
1. Helpful Communication	Weekly worship
2. Holy Conversation	Prayer

---

2 Foss, Michael, *Power Surge,* Fortress Press, 2000.

3. Healthy Conflict   Studying Scripture

4. Healing Candor   Giving

5. Humbled Confidence   Serving

6. Hope-filled Collaboration   Spiritual friendship.

Now that you know what to expect, let's begin this journey together. We will start with ground school in Part One, continue learning and flight training in Part Two, and launch leaders in the final section. Let's take flight together!

CHAPTER ONE
Helpful Communication

"William Dean Howells, editor of 'The Atlantic Monthly,' had written that the people of Ohio were the sort of idealists who had 'the courage of their dreams.' By this courage they have made the best of them come true, and it is well for them in their mainly matter-of-fact and practical character that they show themselves at times enthusiasts and even fanatics."[3]

We are inundated with information. Helpful communication clarifies. Helpful communication inspires. Helpful communication is planned.

If we are to grow as leaders, examining our helpful communication is a good starting place.

Leaders make a habit of helpful communication. Unhelpful communication confuses. Unhelpful communication breeds mediocrity and stasis. Unhelpful communication needs constant clarification.

Helpful communication gives us enough direction to make decisions without always having to check back. Helpful communication fortifies the courage of dreams. Gutsy

---

3 McCullough, David. *The Wright Brothers*. (New York City: Simon & Schuster. 2015) Kindle edition, 204-207.

leaders make a habit of helpful communication.

Without a vision, the people perish.

Proverbs 29:18a, KJV

Helpful Communication Clarifies

In trying to defend or justify their actions, people often say, "I erred on the side of . . ."

The person who waited to start a new entrepreneurial venture until they had raised extra capital to protect their business from an unforeseen downturn says, "I erred on the side of caution."

A mother of teenagers might congratulate herself by saying, "I erred on the side of the least drama." The football coach who plays the prevent defense when ahead by two touchdowns tells the post-game press conference that they lost because, "We erred on the side of protecting a lead." Or the pastor who wants to welcome and accept new people proclaims, "I always err on the side of grace. In this church we want to always err on the side of grace."

Helpful communication does not apologize for what it calls people to do, but states clearly the calling and purpose of the work needing to be done.

One does not err on the side of grace. We choose to lead with grace, that is who we are. That is who we aspire to be. Helpful communication states clearly the call to something more.

When I (Phil) was appointed to serve a church in Grayson, Georgia, in my time of listening to God for inspiration, I discovered the phrase, "Grace in Community for the

16

Grayson Community." We chose to lead with grace there. We did not err on the side of grace, for grace is never an error!

At our new member classes, I would share the story of a pastor who was sent to serve a church in midtown Atlanta. Many people thought he was sent there to close the church because numbers had dwindled substantially and "its best days were behind it." On one of his first Sundays, he walked out the front doors of the church to see the Gay Pride Parade coming down Peachtree Street in Atlanta. When he looked across the street at First Baptist Church, Atlanta, he saw armed guards, mounted police, and barricades in response to that parade. The pastor thought to himself, that does not look like the Kingdom of God. Is that a Kingdom response to the Pride Parade? Over the course of the next year, he invited the people of his struggling church to study the scriptures and ask the question, "What would a Kingdom response look like?" The answer came in Matthew:

Whoever welcomes you, welcomes me, and whoever welcomes me welcomes the one who sent me. Whoever welcomes a prophet in the name of a prophet will receive a prophet's reward; and whoever welcomes a righteous person in the name of a righteous person will receive the reward of the righteous; and whoever gives even a cup of cold water to one of these little ones in the name of a disciple – truly I tell you, none of these will lose their reward.

Matthew 10:40-42 (NRSV)

The next year, the remnant of people at that midtown church were sitting and standing out front of the church when the parade made its way past. They handed out cold cups of water in Jesus' name. They held up signs that said,

17

"Everyone is Welcome in God's Church." I said to a new
membership class at Grayson, "We are not here to debate our
perspectives on homosexuality, but I believe the response of
one of those churches looked like the Kingdom of God. If you
are looking for a more judgmental church, you might need to
go somewhere else." We stated clearly who we were aspiring
to be. We chose to lead with grace and not with judgment to
create Grace in Community for the Grayson Community.
People wanted to be a part of that movement. (An Additional
Note: First Baptist, Atlanta, the one with the barricades,
eventually moved out of midtown Atlanta but St. Mark UMC
remained and continues to be a vibrant church serving that
community for Christ.)

Gutsy Leaders Provide Helpful Communication that Clarifies Direction and Purpose.

Helpful communication is an art. How does one find the
balance between too much and too little? Over the years
We have listened to companies and churches tout their core
values. We love the core values of one new church start in
Western North Carolina. Andrea Smith, pastor at West UMC
in Mooresville, NC reminds us that their first core value
is **Jesus**. What a great place to start with your non-nego-
tiables. What could be more helpful than stating emphati-
cally up-front that Jesus is our first core value? Their next
core value is **Relevant**. This team of leaders works to keep
sharing Jesus in ways that are relevant to people's lives
and that is inherently helpful. Their third core value is
gnignahC, which is written backwards or upside down to
remind the people that we are constantly changing, in order
to stay relevant and communicate the message in helpful
ways. A willingness to change is built into their core values

by the way they are written. Their fourth core value is **Fun**. They trust that the joy of the Lord is their strength. While they acknowledge that life is not always fun, they include a playfulness in worship and leading that is compelling. Finally, their fifth core value is **All!** "All!" seeks the radical inclusion of all people into the love of Jesus, a love that can change us all. Gutsy leadership like that at West UMC offers bold core values that are worth sacrificing for.

While these core values have shaped a church culture, we would venture to say that the best core values take it one step further. The most helpful core values have an imperative that calls us to more. For example, David Cummings, founder of Pardot, offers three simple, yet profound, core values that were used to help people work together there. If you were not all three of these, you were not a good fit for their culture:

- Positive

- Supporting

- Self-starting.

When Phil heard David Cummings speak, he added the imperative:

- Be Positive
- Be Supportive
- Be a Self-starter (Take Initiative).

It is a simple yet powerful shift of expectation, allowing us to ask the questions of ourselves:

- Am I being positive in this workplace?
- Am I being supportive of others?
- Am I taking initiative?

Might we ask church leaders to live up to the same values?

- Am I being positive in the way I talk about this church?
- Am I supportive of others in their faith journey?
- Am I taking initiative to help lead the church or the ministry in which I am involved or am I waiting for someone to tell me what to do next?

One of our Bishops said there are three types of team members.

1. The A player is the one who once they know the purpose and direction of the work, takes initiative while doing more than is expected of them. You merely need to have their back and support them when they risk boldly.

2. The B player does a good job with each task assigned but waits for the next task to be assigned rather than

taking initiative.

3. The C player is the team member you need to sit down with and have "that" talk with about their performance. Unfortunately, they have been having that same talk with teachers, parents, and supervisors their whole lives. So, when you sit down with them to have "that" talk, they are better at the talk then you are. They often make you feel bad or even responsible for their lack of initiative or performance.

The clear vision articulated in core values provided direction and gave employees the ability to self-regulate without always having to check in with someone else to see what to do next. This lesson echoes in David Cumming's newest venture, the Atlanta Tech Village, that features their imperative core values on the wall:

• Be nice.
• Dream big.
• Work hard. Play hard.
• Pay it forward.

When you know the core values of your organization, it is easier to be about the task at hand. Too many of our churches have implicit core values but fail to articulate them in a way that guides and regulates behavior. Gutsy leaders articulate and stand by their core values, reinforcing them with their own behavior and telling stories about those who live out the core values in ways that make a difference!

Helpful Communication Inspires

Helpful communication fills the mind with wonder. It causes us to ask questions, to wonder about what might be. Orville and Wilbur Wright, two bicycle mechanics by trade from Dayton, Ohio, learned helpful communication from their father, Milton Wright, a Bishop in the Church of the United Brethren in Christ. Bishop Wright was a straightforward man with high standards. "At home he (Bishop Wright) preached courage and good character – 'good mettle,' as he

22

would say – worthy purpose, and perseverance. Providing guidelines he understood to be part of a father's duty." [4]

Bishop Wright stressed the importance of hard work to his boys and gifted them with the joy of reading. They learned helpful communication by both listening to him and reading his letters from his travels on behalf of the church. Yet, Bishop Wright was not afraid of playfulness. He believed in the educational value of toys. Not realizing this simple act would one day change the world, he brought home a toy helicopter from France, which the boys later said began their fascination with flying. It was merely a stick with propeller and a twisted rubber band but the boys saw something more. From their mother, Susan Koerner Wright, they inherited the ability to work with their hands. It was said that she was "a 'regular genius' in that she could make anything, and toys especially, even a sled, 'as good as a store kind.'"[5] The boys played with that toy helicopter they called "the bat" and when it broke, they figured out how to fix it. Pretty soon they were making their own versions. Even in class at school, a teacher would find them tinkering with materials or drawing sketches of flying machines.

Orville and Wilbur Wright were visionary leaders. They had a vision that human beings would one day fly. Others shared that vision and were more heavily funded, but these two were able to accomplish something that connected us across the world. They made plan after plan of how to create a machine that would take us to the air. They began to communicate that vision to others. This vision for "what might be" guided their lives. How they would get there was

---

4 McCullough, *The Wright Brothers*, 224-225.

5 McCullough, *The Wright Brothers*, 124-125.

up for debate, and debate they did, within the safety of deep brotherly love.

When Orville became ill, Wilbur read to him aloud about two brothers in Germany, the Lilienthals, who had tried to mimic the flight of birds using gliders to take to the air. Learning that two brothers had already worked on this issue together and that one of those brothers had died trying to fly further inspired Orville and Wilbur. They became convinced that not only was flight possible but also that the beautiful flight of birds held the answers for how we might be able to soar as well.

Helpful communication helps us to see what is not yet. The Wright brothers' toy bat helped them to see a vision for the future. They had heard about flight, but actually seeing it took their dreams and plans to a new level. The simple "bat" communicated to them a world of possibilities for now they had "seen" it. Helpful communication paints a vision for us even when we ourselves cannot yet see it. Helpful communication paints a vision for others to see that which is not yet. One of the Lilienthal brothers died trying to make winged flight a reality. A compelling vision calls us to take risks. Gutsy leaders are willing to take those risks, to sacrifice safety to accomplish something greater.

Noted rabbi and author Edwin Friedman expressed that people can't think their way out of their problems, that our problems cannot be solved by more thinking. He stated that it is only through adventure that we can expand our understanding in order to find new categories in which to discover solutions. For the Wright brothers, a simple toy was the beginning of that adventure, but reading and experimenting allowed them to bring their vision into being. The Lilienthal brothers had spent very few hours in actual flight.

They were on the right track trying to understand the flight of birds but it was not until Orville and Wilbur actually practiced imitating birds that they learned the limitations of others' research. Experts who had been experimenting with winged flight had published standard calculations that those pursuing manned flight generally assumed were correct. It was not until Wilbur and Orville did their own experiments that they realized the conventional wisdom was misguided. They took the risk of ridicule by creating their flying machine based on their own calculations and experimentation rather than based upon the agreed upon standard of the so-called experts who preceded them. In their experiments with flight, the Wright brothers knew there would be risks so they made a rule to never fly together, because they always wanted someone to be there to carry on the work. Helpful communication calls others to carry on the work!

Helpful Communication Inspires Action

Gary McIntosh in his book, Staffing Your Church for Growth, identifies actions that help churches to grow and actions that help churches to decline. Finding new people, keeping people connected, and celebrating with people are actions seen in growing churches. In declining churches, pastors and leaders find themselves caring for people rather than helping them care for others, supervising people rather than giving them the accountable guidelines in which to lead and serve, and educating people so they know more about the Bible and the traditions of the faith rather than actually putting the lessons learned into practice as everyday disciples. Many of our churches stress the importance of education but if the result of education is merely acquisition of knowledge rather than information that leads to action, our communication has been interesting but not all that helpful. Gutsy leadership not only inspires, but inspires action!

In working with one of our new church starts in the Atlanta area, I (Phil) clearly stated to the clergy couple who was beginning this endeavor that I wanted them each to meet twenty new people in their community every week, and to send me the names of those they met so I could pray for those people. Their coach pushed it one step further and challenged them to have six one-on-ones the next week with people they had met who seemed open to further conversation. In those follow-up meetings, they were charged with hearing the person's story and asking, "Who else in this community do I need to meet?" After about ten weeks of connecting with new people in their community, this young couple called to say they wanted to see me. I started to run through in my mind all the things they could want to talk about. When we sat down, they asked, "Why didn't you tell us about this 'twenty new people a week' thing earlier in our ministries? It would have changed our churches. It would have changed our communities. It is already changing us as we are new to the community, but we are the ones introducing neighbors to each other." This new church is taking seriously the call of finding new people. Helpfully communicating the vision calls people to action.

Helpful communication makes ideas take flight!

Helpful communication is planned.

First Things First - Planning that Gives Direction

Ever worried about starting something new? A new job? A new venture?

When faced with starting a new position several years

ago, a colleague, Rev. Tom Davis of Roswell UMC in Georgia, told Phil he needed to read Stephen Covey's *First Things First.*[6] Covey offered a simple chart that guided Phil's entire time in that position and still continues to guide him today. Covey stated simply that there are things in life that are urgent and things in life that are not urgent. There are things in life that are important and things that are not important. When something is urgent, it demands our immediate attention. When something is important it can have a lasting impact.

	Urgent	Not Urgent
Important		
Not Important		

Covey correctly asserted that we are addicted to the urgent rather than being driven by the important. When something is urgent and important, it's a Crisis - it demands our immediate attention.

	Urgent	Not Urgent
Important	Crisis	
Not Important		

When the presenting issue is neither urgent nor important, Covey calls that **Waste**. We have all found ourselves wasting time in task avoidance. Waste can be all too easy to identify.

---

6 Covey, Merrill, and Merrill, *First Things First,* Free Press, January 17, 1996.

	Urgent	Not Urgent
Important	Crisis	
Not Important		Waste

When something is Urgent, but Not Important, that is when we are in a time of Deception. We are deceiving ourselves, allowing our addiction to the urgent to dictate our time and attention. This is much harder to spot but results when someone else who does not share our vision dictates the use of our time and our priority. It used to be the ringing phone that called us away from the task we thought was important. Today it is email, which is essentially someone else's to-do list sent to you. When you allow someone else's urgency (when they are not your boss) to guide how you spend your time, you are in the deception zone. You may be busy but you will not be able to transform the system or yourself.

	Urgent	Not Urgent
Important	Crisis	
Not Important	Deception	Waste

Covey then asks the question, "What one thing, if you did it with excellence, would most improve your professional life?" (He asks us to examine our personal lives, too, with a similar question. "What one thing, if you did it with excellence, would most improve your personal life?")

Phil sat and pondered his response. Just one thing? There are so many to choose from.

Take a moment to write down your answer. Don't over-think it. What response comes to mind first? "What one thing, if you did it with excellence, would most improve your professional life or your work?"

My simple response was, "I need to plan further in advance." I needed to take time away so that I could listen for God's direction. Then when I returned, I would be more able to clearly articulate where I felt God was leading us. Answering this question forces you to identify what would bring more Quality to your life. We know it is true but we tend not to invest in quality with the urgent tugging at our sleeves.

Too often we run from crisis to crisis, never spending time in the deep work needed to really change a system or be changed ourselves. In order to live in the quality quadrant, I had to plan further in advance. I had to spend time investing in quality and when I did, I found that the other three quadrants shrank. I spent less time in crisis, less time in deception, and far less time in waste. In those times when I missed the quality quadrant, I found myself back in crisis mode as that quadrant grew and grew. If you know what would most improve your life, then why aren't you doing it?

	Urgent	Not Urgent
Important	Crisis	**Quality**
Not Important	Deception	Waste

Helpful communication takes planning because it's role is to provide direction. Helpful communication tells us where we are headed. Taking time to listen to God before charging off in a direction can change us and the systems in which we live and work.

When we fail to plan far enough in advance, we keep other people out of the creative process. As we travel from church to church, we see our healthiest churches plan far enough into the future so that others can take the journey and impact how the journey is completed through holy conversation.

Have you ever walked into a team or committee meeting that lacked direction? Once the direction has been established people can participate more fully. Leadership articulates direction through helpful communication. In the Biblical record, vision seems to be given to individuals like Moses, Peter, and others. But that vision must be confirmed by the community. Lovett Weems expresses the idea that vision is given to a community, but the leader is often the first to discern and then articulate where we are headed. Once direction is set, then the team edits how we get there through holy conversation and healthy conflict. Helpful communication gives us the boundaries we need to start the conversation about the "How." When there is trust that comes from holy conversation, we can engage in healthy conflict to get to the best solution of our "How" so we can live into the vision without division.

We begin this leadership journey with the concept of helpful communication. Helpful communication steers our thinking like the front wheel of a bicycle. Helpful communication inspires action and causes people to strive to dream of something more. Helpful communication leads to holy conversation.

CHAPTER TWO
Holy Conversation

Holy conversation doesn't just happen. Holy conversation starts with the right questions.

Holy conversation builds trust. If we are to grow as leaders, we must be open to God's leading, leading us into holier conversations than the ones we have been having.

Unholy conversation is mean-spirited. Unholy conversation leaves a wake. Unholy conversation undermines our witness. Unholy conversation is easy, too easy. Unholy conversation undermines relationships and undermines trust.

Holy conversation starts with preparation, preparing to hear the voice of God through another.

Holy conversation requires an intention to listen for what is said and not said. Holy conversation trusts the Holy Spirit to intervene in our interactions. Holy conversation involves an openness to something beyond ourselves and our agendas.

Leaders Make a Habit of Holy Conversation.

When the Lord saw that he had turned aside to see,
God called to him out of the bush, "Moses, Moses!"
And he said, "Here I am." Then he said, "Come no
closer! Remove the sandals from your feet, for the
place on which you are standing is holy ground."

Exodus 3:4-5 (NRSV)

Holy Conversation Doesn't Just Happen

Homiletics professor, Dr. Fred Craddock, used to say you can't invite someone to join you for a "meaningful breakfast." You just invite them to breakfast. Then you invite them to breakfast again and again. As you get to know one another better, building trust and sharing stories, some of the breakfasts become meaningful. It is like spending quality time with your kids or others you love. The only way you have quality time with them is by spending more and more time with them. We cannot force something to be quality time just because we say it is going to be. Quality time comes in fits and spurts, breaking in occasionally through countless hours of interaction. In fact, when we don't spend time with our children or people we love, hoping and praying for the time to be quality, the crisis quadrant can grow in our lives and theirs.

Holy conversation doesn't just happen. Someone has to take the initiative to create a setting in which people can discuss where they are headed and how best to get to that destination. When a vision has been established, healthy leaders invite holy conversation around that vision. Gutsy leaders are not afraid to listen to the voice of God, directly and from others. One of my colleagues leads his team with

32

these words, "group process." He constantly and consistently stresses group process. He knows he has a tendency to run ahead so he values holy conversation to keep the group functioning at its best. In order to build a leadership team, he stresses group process with his lay and staff teams. This group process is the setting for holy conversation. They listen for the voice of God together in prayer and then openly discuss and debate whatever issue is at hand. People often try to circumvent that process, running ahead or around the group, which undermines transparency and trust. This gutsy leader continues to call the team back to holy conversation, seeking to make better decisions together. The group processing is slower at first, but people learn to trust the wisdom of the group. Building trust takes these kinds of face-to-face interactions. It is here we learn to trust each other's intentions when we are not in the group setting.

"Judge others by their intentions, judge yourself by your actions."

Hal Brady, Senior Pastor of Glenn Memorial UMC
(at the time of the quote)

A new biography of Supreme Court Justice Sandra Day O'Connor by Evan Thomas records how Justice O'Connor thought it was essential to encourage collegiality between the justices. She fostered this by trying to get more justices to gather together for weekly lunches. When she began this practice, less than half the justices would join her. Her biographer told National Public Radio that "O'Connor would show up in missing justices' chambers and sit there until they came with her." It did not matter to her what the justices' underlying ideologies were, she believed the shared meal would strengthen the team as they sought to interpret the law and rule justly. In 1991, when Justice Clarence Thomas joined the court he failed to respond to her numerous invitations, but she persevered. She went and sat outside his office week after week, waiting for him, until he finally joined them. We can assume it was not always "holy conversation" but we suspect there were kairotic moments where the discussions took on a transcendent quality.[7]

Patrick Lencioni in his book, *The Five Dysfunctions of a Team,*[8] argues that the absence of trust leads to a fear of conflict and a lack of commitment. Yet, trust seems to be built by committing to one another. Because the justices committed to weekly lunches, the shared table fellowship allowed them to break down barriers and begin to create a level of trust across differences. Might committing to spend time together with a sense of openness be the first step toward holy conversation?

In North Georgia, I (Phil) have the privilege of working in the Center for Congregational Excellence which offers training and consulting for local churches. In gathering our Congregational Excellence team here in North Georgia, the newest members of the team asked, "What exactly is our role?" My quick response was, "Our work is to make the life of pastor and lay leaders in local churches easier, and if not easier, better." Our team is there as a resource to local churches to bring training where needed and connection to other churches who are already doing things well. Over the

---

7 Weiss, Debra Cassen. "Upcoming Sandra Day O'Connor biography reveals her opinion on Alito, outreach to Thomas." Abajournal.com. http://www.abajournal.com/news/article/upcoming-sandra-day-oconnor-biography-reveals-her-opinion-on-alito-outreach-to-thomas. Accessed May 14, 2019.

8 Lencioni, Patrick, *The Five Dysfunctions of a Team,* Jossey-Bass, 2002.

past year, our team has gathered for conversation around this vision of what we are trying to accomplish. There have been holy moments where flashes of insight have helped us direct our work. One image continues to echo: we seek to be a church's "pit crew." We are not racing ourselves, but we are there to support the work of those running the race set before them, like a great team of airplane or bicycle mechanics.

One local church in South Georgia, Harvest in Warner Robbins, has offered a great teaching tool in their Sunday afternoon follow-up email to visitors:

> *It was really good to have you at Harvest this week. I hope you enjoyed the service. I don't know if you're looking for answers, a church home, or just passing through. Whatever the case, I'm glad you chose to check us out. We think church should be a fun, practical place to get the answers we need for life and help us grow in a relationship with God. Helping people connect with God is what Harvest is all about.*
>
> *By the way, as a first-time guest, you have a special point of view that we are always interested in: What was your first impression?*
>
> *Would you take a minute to complete this short, 4-question, survey? We want Harvest to have a warm and comfortable atmosphere for our guests, so, your input will really help.*

Harvest First Impressions

1. What was your first impression of Harvest?

2. What did you enjoy most?

3. *How did you find out about Harvest?*

Billboard

Car Magnet

Internet/Website

Invited by family, friend, or co-worker

Newspaper

Postcard

Radio

Other:

4. *Other Comments?*

The vision for the church is right there in the email, "We think church should be **a fun practical place to get the answers we need for life and help us grow in a relationship with God. Helping people connect with God** is what Harvest is all about."

Rather than just sending a first-time visitor information about the church, they open up the door for holy conversation, for the visitor to give them feedback to help strengthen the church. The visitor's input is welcome from the very beginning, thus making the visitor a part of the church's mission from the very first day. Holy conversation can happen when leaders invite candid feedback. When using a first-time visitor survey like this in the local church consider adding a fifth question, "What are you praying for?"

Holy Conversation Starts with the Right Questions

Early in my ministry, I (Phil) felt like prayer was often used as an escape hatch to get out of situations. I had been in a hospital room for an extended time visiting a parish-

ioner so I would suggest a prayer. Never did I have anyone
say "no." I would pray and then exit. At some level, I felt
as though I was imposing my prayer on them or at least
what I thought we should be praying for. I discussed this
struggle with my teaching parish group, a group of trusted
colleagues who were also students learning about ministry
in the context of small rural churches. As we debated the
pros and cons of praying as pastoral care in homes and
hospital rooms, I wondered aloud, "What if instead of
imposing prayer or just asking can I pray for you, I asked
people, 'What are you praying for?'" This was different from
"How can I pray for you?" The question allowed me to guide
them on their own reflections. The question changed the
responses. Occasionally a person would say, "What am I
praying for? I have to admit, I really don't pray," or "I don't
really know how to pray." This opened up an opportunity for
teaching, discipleship, and more holy conversations.

I remember sitting in the home of one young couple and
asking, "What are you praying for?" They went silent,
sharing knowing looks back and forth. Finally, the husband
asked, "Should we tell him?" She nodded that they should.
He began to share about the series of miscarriages they had
been through and just didn't know where else to turn. They
decided to come visit a church. They were praying to have
a child and they were talking to a pastor who was a fertility
baby, whose parents had tried for 10 years to have him! They
were talking to the pastor of a church that had just started a
new Sunday school class. What did many in that class have
in common with each other? Issues of fertility and stories
of adoption. In fact, one of the couples had joined the church
after our third Sunday in Advent Celebration of Adoption
Sunday, a tribute to Joseph and his willingness to adopt

Jesus as his own. Their answer to that question changed our closing minutes together from a surface level prayer and goodbye into a holy conversation. Holy conversations require us to be vulnerable so there is room enough for God in our deliberations. Hearing what people are praying for is literally a holy conversation.

Nina Reeves, beloved storyteller from North Alabama, has a habit of sitting down for a meal with people she hasn't seen in a while and saying, "First, let us now speak of the deepest things we know." She knows that there are many things we could talk about but she invokes the holy in those conversations by directing us to consider the deepest things we know first. Holy conversation excavates, searching for the deepest things we know, taking our discussions to a whole new level. This habit of speaking of the deepest things first could help us avoid much unholy talk. Too often we start our table conversations with the easiest things we know, perhaps that is why it is called "small talk."

As churches are trying to find new ways to reach new people, some churches have started the concept of "dinner church" where people gather around a meal for what is hoped to be holy conversation. One of our local churches in North Georgia has started a dinner church twice a month where people are invited for free food, music, and a message of hope. A Jesus' story of good news is shared with the group, then people talk about the story over a meal. They reflect together and discuss the implications of the message for their lives.[9]

My wife, Elizabeth, and I decided to try that on a smaller

---

9   Douglasville Dinner Church. https://www.facebook.com/DouglasvilleDinnerChurch/. Accessed May 13, 2019.

scale. We posted to Facebook that we would be hosting a dinner church in our home. Would anyone be interested in joining us for a meal and a discussion of some good news? Before the day was over, we had twelve people who had signed up. They gathered in our home, some who knew each other beforehand, some who did not. One of our guests shared a scripture and gave us some questions to discuss around the dinner table. We fixed our plates and drifted into small talk but then we considered the deeper things as we discussed the questions raised around the scripture. The conversation shifted quickly as one of those present began to share a story of deep pain, loss, and disappointment. The table fellowship allowed for that holy conversation to occur as we took the time to really listen to each other in response to the prompting of scripture.

Holy Conversation Builds Trust

Orville and Wilbur Wright trusted each other with a great depth which came out of their commitment to their purpose and love for each other as brothers. When one brother, Orville was suffering from typhoid in 1896, at the age of twenty-five his brother Wilbur, sat by his bedside nursing him back to health reading. Perhaps, some holy conversation comes when one person talks and the other listens attentively. Holy conversation happens when we listen attentively for the voice of God.

David McCullough paints the scene in this way:

It was a month before Orville could sit up in bed, another two weeks before he could get out of bed, and during this time Wilbur had begun reading about the German glider enthusiast Otto Lilienthal who

had recently been killed in an accident. Much that he read he read aloud to Orville. A manufacturer of small steam engines and a mining engineer by training, Lilienthal had started gliding as early as 1869, and from the start he had been joined in his aviation experiments by a younger brother, which could only have given Wilbur and Orville a feeling of something in common. He took his lessons from the birds, Lilienthal said, and he saw, as many "prominent investigators" had not, that the secret of "the art of flight" was to be found in the arched or vaulted wings of birds, by which they could ride the wind. He had no use for gas balloons as a means of flight, as they had nothing in common with the birds. "What we are seeking is the means of free motion in the air, in any direction." And only by flying oneself could one achieve "proper insight" into all that was involved. To do this, one had to be on "intimate" terms with the wind.[10]

This time of reading and holy listening changed the course of history. They realized together that they had to fly themselves in order to really understand the flight of birds, to be on intimate terms with the wind, with the Holy Spirit flowing through them, allowing them to have holy conversations about the direction their experiments would take them.

One of my most gifted colleagues once asked me, "Would you be willing to tell me something about myself that I need to know but that you might be afraid to tell me for fear of hurting my feelings?" I was astonished. I did a double-take. "You want me to do what? You want me to tell you a truth about you from my perspective? This seems like a dangerous act." He reassured me that he had been doing some soul-searching and some wise counsel had challenged him to

---

10 McCullough, *The Wright Brothers*, 391-403.

ask that question of people he respected. I took a deep breath and told him that his public speaking often felt more like the reading of prepared written remarks rather than speaking that was prepared for the ear. He seemed to prepare more to be read than to be heard. I waited for him to punch me, but he thanked me for my honesty and agreed to work through my feedback. His openness and vulnerability allowed me to ask him the same question. I still hear his answer echo at times when I fall prey to what he identified. He said, "You often get ahead of the rest of us and assume we know what you are thinking or how you got to your conclusions. If you could slow down and bring the rest of us along it would help you and help us."

Walter Wangerin revealed the gift of such mirrors of Holy Conversation in his book *Reliving the Passions:*

> In mirrors I see myself. But in mirrors made of glass and silver I never see the whole of myself. I see the me I want to see, and I ignore the rest. Mirrors that hide nothing hurt me. They reveal an ugliness I'd rather deny. Yow! Avoid these mirror of veracity! My wife is such a mirror. When I have sinned against her, my sin appears in the suffering of her face. Her tears reflect with terrible accuracy my selfishness. My self! But I hate the sight, and the same selfishness I see now makes me look away. "Stop crying!" I command, as though the mirror were at fault. Or else I just leave the room. Walk away. Oh, what a coward I am, and what a fool! Only when I have the courage fully to look, clearly to know myself – will I admit my need for healing. But if I look away from her whom I have hurt, I have also turned away from her who might forgive me. I reject the very source of my healing. My denial of my sin protects, preserves, perpetuates that sin! Ugliness in me, while I live in illusions, can only grow the uglier. Mirrors that hide nothing hurt me. But

this is the hurt of purging and precious renewal – and these are the mirrors of dangerous grace.

Gutsy leaders are not afraid to look in the mirror and to listen to the holy conversation that ensues in their internal reflection. Gutsy leaders appreciate the mirrors provided by others.

Transitions Open Opportunity for Holy Conversation

Times of transition can be especially vulnerable times. People want to get off on the right foot and make a good first impression. In an itinerant system of pastoral deployment, one would think churches and denominational leaders would give concerted effort to making the time of starting ministry at a new church as effective as possible. Claire Bowen, a layperson at one of our large churches had been on-boarding new leaders in the business and non-profit world for years. She suggested to her pastor that had she done that for him when he started, he would have been six months ahead in information and insight in a twenty-four-hour period. Since she had not done it for him, he suggested that she do it for a colleague moving to a church in another state. She agreed. The pastor testified that this on-boarding process saved him countless hours and meetings and put him a year ahead of where he would have been without it.

On-boarding consists of a half-day of questions and a half-day of responses. It invites holy conversation quickly. A new leader invites a trained on-boarding consultant to come spend a day with the staff of the church. The leader introduces the on-boarder, implores the staff to be as honest as possible, prays for them, and leaves. The on-boarder then asks a series of questions of the staff designed to bring all their questions and concerns about the transition to the surface. What do you know about this new leader? What do you wish you knew about them? What worries you about this transition? Each answer is recorded to be shared with the incoming leader that evening, but the source of each data point is not revealed. The answers are anonymous but not confidential. The data will be shared but not attributed. After a time of coaching, the new leader stands before their new team and responds to each piece of data so that everyone on the team hears the same answers at the same time. This avoids having to have similar conversations with everyone on staff over a period of weeks. The new leader gets on board quickly and knows more about their new setting in day than they could discover in six months of individual discussions.

STOP

Because it is so easy to slip into unholy conversation, one of our colleagues offers a standard operating procedure (STOP) for his staff and lay leaders. When he was moved to a new church, he found constant triangulation of the staff by members of the church. Rather than talking directly to people, he found most interactions involved talking about people. He challenged his staff to take on a new habit. Whenever someone started talking about someone else, he would stop them and say, "I know _____ to be a fine person, and when you talk to them, they will be glad to listen." This phrase became a staff norm. Whenever someone started a conversation with a person not present in the room, a member of the staff would state, "I know _____ to be a fine person and when you talk to them, they will be glad to listen." It became an automatic response. In fact, it became such of part of the church's culture that halfway through someone complaining about someone who was not present, they would stop themselves and say, "I know what you are going to say. 'They are a fine person' and I should go talk with them about my issue rather than talking to you about them." Not only is it Biblical but also it is how we form strong teams and stronger cultures in our churches and beyond. When we listen to someone's complaint, they often think we agree with them. The senior pastor at this church argued that people needed a prepared response, because under stress we can forget our best intentions. This habit of redirection fostered growth and minimized unhealthy conversations. Where could you or your team benefit from having an automatic response that edifies? At least at one church this has become an almost automatic response and much unholy conversation has been avoided.

If another member of the church sins against you, go and point out the fault when the two of you are alone. If the member listens to you, you have regained that one.

Matthew 18:15 (NRSV)

Holy conversation doesn't just happen, it takes work and preparation. Holy conversation starts with the right questions while listening to God and others. Holy conversation builds trust in a face-to-face group process.

Helpful communication sets direction. Holy conversation allows us to discuss how we get to where we're are going. Holy conversation opens the door for healthy conflict that allows us to move beyond "nice" to that which is "necessary."

CHAPTER THREE

Healthy Conflict

Jesus never asked anyone to play it safe.
We were born to be brave.

Bob Goff, Author of *Love Does* via Twitter

Healthy conflict moves us beyond our own insecurities. Healthy conflict comes from a heart at peace. Healthy conflict allows people to be heard. Healthy conflict speaks the truth in love. If we want to grow as leaders, we must be willing to engage in healthy conflict.

Unhealthy conflict is laced with hostility emanating from our anxiety. Unhealthy conflict comes from a heart at war. Unhealthy conflict stifles conversation. Unhealthy conflict is blaming and accusatory.

Healthy conflict based in love bears all things, believes all things, endures all things. Gutsy leaders make a habit of healthy conflict.

One of our now deceased pastors in NGA and former director of Congregation Development, Rev. Clay Jacobs, was trying to help one of our young pastors who was facing conflict at his church as he was pushing them to more fully engage the community. Clay told the young pastor, "There's incredible creative tension in the midst of conflict. Don't avoid conflict, it's an opportunity for creativity and growth."

You must get along with each other, you must learn to be considerate of one another cultivating a life in common.
I Corinthians 1:10 (MSG)

Healthy Conflict Moves Us Beyond Our Own Insecurities

In July of 1957, John Lennon and Paul McCartney met in church of all places. John Lennon and his group, the Quarrymen, were playing at the Grand Hall of St. Peter's Church in Liverpool. Paul McCartney listened to them play and was impressed by Lennon's creative musicianship. John didn't seem to know all the words to the song he was singing but substituted the words of an old blues song on the spot in a way that worked. The story is told that Paul taught John how to tune his guitar before Paul played a couple of songs that night as well. Some considered that Paul's audition. The Quarrymen soon met and discussed whether to add Paul to their group. John Lennon was a bit intimidated, worrying that Paul's talent might overshadow his and challenge his leadership in the group. The Quarrymen engaged in a bit of healthy conflict around the table but the real conflict was within John's own mind. Could he handle having this younger, perhaps superior, musician in the group? John finally worked through his own insecurity and decided it was in the best interest of the group to ask Paul to join. Paul pondered the invitation and eventually decided to join The Quarrymen. Three years later, they became The Beatles.

46

Examine One's Own Heart and Mind

Healthy conflict begins by examining our internal response, within one's own heart and mind. As the people of the Arbinger Institute point out, when a person is not in touch with their own feelings, what starts as a disagreement can easily lead to the other person being seen as disagreeable which escalates the conflict beyond its original scope.

Healthy conflict concentrates on the issue of disagreement rather than making the other person the problem. Orville and Wilbur Wright often fought about ideas and the best way to bring their dream of flying to fruition, but the trust they had constructed while growing up together kept them from demonizing each other over disagreements about process or style. Healthy conflict is a practice of being able to see the other person's position clearly even when there is not agreement on how to resolve the tension between seemingly contradictory positions. The Wright brothers fought like committed siblings; they were not leaving the relationship over disagreement which is a key to healthy conflict.

Everything considered, they got along well, each aware of what the other brought to the task at hand, each long familiar with the other's particular nature, and always with the unspoken understanding that Wilbur, the older by four years, was the senior member of the partnership, the big brother. Not that things always went smoothly. They could be highly demanding and critical of each other, disagree to the point of shouting "something terrible." At times, after an hour or more of heated argument, they would find themselves as far from agreement as when they started, except that each had changed to the other's original position. As

47

often said, neither ever chose to be anything other than himself, a quality that rated high in Ohio. Not only did they have no yearning for the limelight, they did their best to avoid it. And with the onset of fame, both remained notably modest.[11]

One of my (Phil) Course of Study students at the Candler School of Theology once said, "Instead of churches growing and maturing, they change pastors. And instead of pastors growing and maturing, they change churches." In an itinerant system like The United Methodist Church, there is less incentive to push through conflict into a new healthier reality. It may be easier to move on to the next place and start over, which results in the same type of conflicts merely being repeated in new settings. Healthy conflict begins with internal wrestling, asking yourself, do you really want things to be better or do you just want them to be different? If you want them to be better, you stay and engage in healthy conflict.

I (Phil) once served a church that had been dealing with one family who perpetually stirred up controversy and conflict. Their communication was less than helpful and their conversation was seldom holy. One of their perennial tactics was to get close to the pastor and the pastor's family. They would then take anything less than positive they learned about the pastor and spin it back through the congregation in destructive ways. They would ask the pastor's children intrusive questions about the pastor. After several months at the church, several members came to me and asked, "What are you going to do about this family and their devious actions?" This family had been in conflict with every pastor that served that church in recent years. These concerned members were surprised when I said, "I'm

---

11 McCullough, *The Wright Brothers*, 102-109.

not going to do anything about that family." The concerned members pushed me - wasn't I concerned about this family undermining my leadership and the church? I responded that it wasn't my church. It was ultimately God's church and for the time being, their church. They would be dealing with that family long after I was gone. It was their responsibility to confront these recalcitrant members who were undermining the health of the church. I finally said, "You are upset with this family about their behavior. If you don't address it, this will be the story of your church long into the future." They so wanted me to be the one to deal with this issue. I pointed out that other former pastors had attempted to take this family on and then moved soon thereafter. I said, "If you want your church to be healthy, you will have to challenge their behavior. Otherwise, they will just wait me out and do this to the next pastor and the pastor after that."

As you might suspect, no one was brave enough to confront this family. Everyone was afraid of them, knowing their wrath could just as easily be pointed toward a church member as towards the pastor. But then, two young women enrolled in a Disciple Bible Study class entitled Becoming Disciples Through Bible Study. They read the scriptures and encountered the living Christ in the text. They read Paul's letters where he took on problems in the church directly. Emboldened by their study and discernment, these two young women thought it was part of their growing discipleship to keep their church healthy. They were maturing in their faith through disciplined study. They went to the family and told them their behavior was unbefitting of a Christian. They told the family they could either "get happy" or leave the church. The two women could no longer stand by and watch someone undermine the church from the inside out. The confronted family was angry! How could anyone talk to them this way? They tried to rally support from other church members, but little was forthcoming. Most people were so proud of these two young women for standing up to these bullies.

The loudest voice in the family left the church and joined a small congregation nearby where he could continue to throw his weight around. The church he left went on to growth and health. It is not easy to engage in healthy conflict but it offers a path to personal spiritual growth and church growth as well.

It reminds me of a consult I (Phil) did in a church about finances and stewardship. Part way through the consultation, a man from the congregation stood up and pointedly told me, "You don't know anything about money. I've raised millions of dollars professionally over the years and you don't know what you are talking about." I was stunned and tried to probe for understanding. His level of anger could not be explained by the preceding conversation. After he stomped out of the meeting, I continued teaching about stewardship practices for the local church. When the meeting was over, person after person came up to me and apologized for his behavior. "I'm sorry he treated you like that." "I'm sorry for what he said to you." After several apologies, I said aloud to those who were still gathered, "Could I have your attention for a moment? Many of you have come up to me and apologized for one of your members' behavior but none of you put a stop to it while he was yelling at me. You say you are sorry for his behavior, but I think you must like it. He plays a role here in your church and you are willing to tolerate his bad behavior. I suspect it will continue." Now they were stunned. I wanted to be candid with them and engage them in healthy conflict. I asked them if this is the kind of church they wanted to be a part of, where an invited guest gets berated for sharing information. Their response was a unanimous, "No!"

One person did retort, "But he is the only man in our choir." I invited them to consider a women's chorus. I invited them to consider what they were going to do about his behavior in the future. We prayed that they would be willing to offer a firm, yet kind, response to him.

Turns out this man had just recently lost his fundraising job, so I suspect his anger was a projection of his grief over his job loss. Even worse, it was revealed that he and his wife were trying to get the church to close so they could rent out the space as a community center. That couple left the church not long after that because they received a letter from the District Superintendent asking them to leave the church for actively trying to undermine the health of the ministry there. I had not seen that before and have not since. Healthy conflict tries not to escalate, but tries to deal with an issue at the level it presents itself.

Churches, pastors, laypersons, and teams that are unwilling or unable to engage in healthy conflict cannot grow and mature. Healthy conflict gets us unstuck! Healthy conflict is like lifting weights - the tearing at the muscle fiber then grows back stronger in the long run. Orville and Wilbur Wright had engaged in brotherly healthy conflict for so long, their agreement about a solution to one of their problems felt odd to them and those gathered around. They were willing to examine the weak points of anything which made their solutions stronger, but it didn't always win them friends.

The letter was dated October 2. That night, as Orville later told the story, discussion in camp on aeronautical theory went on at such length that he indulged himself in more coffee than usual. Unable to sleep, he lay awake

51

thinking about ways to achieve an even better system of control when suddenly he had an idea: the rear rudder, instead of being in a fixed position, should be hinged— movable. In the morning at breakfast, he proposed the change, but not before giving Lorin a wink, a signal to watch Wilbur for one of his customary critical responses. Wilbur, as George Spratt once told Octave Chanute, was "always ready to oppose an idea expressed by anybody," ready to "jump into an argument with both sleeves rolled up." And as Wilbur himself would explain to Spratt, he believed in "a good scrap." It brought out "new ways of looking at things," helped "round off the corners." It was characteristic of all his family, Wilbur said, to be able to see the weak points of anything. This was not always a "desirable quality," he added, "as it makes us too conservative for successful business men, and limits our friendships to a very limited circle." This time, however, after a moment when no one spoke, Wilbur declared he liked the idea, then surprised Orville even more: Why not simplify the pilot's job by connecting control of the rudder with those of the wing warping? Work began on the change that same day.[12]

Where might you and your church benefit from some healthy discussion and conflict?

Healthy Conflict Comes from a Heart at Peace

There is a difference between conflict and hostility. In the church, we often avoid conflict because we have not separated it from hostility which many feel is inherently un-Jesus like, despite the clearing of the moneychangers from the temple. Even Jesus became angry and frustrated at times but he did not shy away from conflict when it mattered. Jesus stood up for what was right, even as it caused conflict

---

12 McCullough, *The Wright Brothers*, 78-79.

and cost him his life, but it was world-changing. Jesus maintained a heart at peace even to the end.

> *"Father forgive them for they know not what they are doing."*
>
> **Luke 23:34 (NRSV)**

Conflict moves us to better decision making. Hostility seeks to wound and to win. Jesus wasn't seeking to wound but to heal a broken system. He consistently challenged the Pharisees about their stance on the law. Was humankind made for the sabbath or the sabbath for humankind?

Conflict can be done with a heart at peace, while hostility proceeds from a heart at war. Heart at war means that we are closed by our own position or beliefs, and we are not willing to compromise or listen to anything contrary. Our actions are to defend, protect, and conquer. A heart at war means that our souls are restless and unsettled, and we are willing to aggressively enforce our beliefs. When we have a heart at war, we see people as objects, and we treat them as vehicles that we use, obstacles that we blame, and irrelevancies that we ignore.

In contrast, a heart at peace means that we know where we stand, but with a "convicted humility," we are open to explore all sides of an issue in order to be open to where God is leading us. Our actions are to be curious, open-minded, and willing to say, "I might be wrong about this." When we have a heart at peace, we see people as subjects, and we seek to know their needs, concerns, and challenges. We treat them with the love and compassion that we yearn to receive from others.[13]

---

13 Hagiya, Bishop Grant. "A Heart at Peace." https://www.ministrymatters.com/all/entry/9169/a-heart-at-peace. September 4, 2018.

When we are in the midst of conflict, we must first ask ourselves several questions. What is going on with me? How am I feeling as we are having these discussions? Is my heart at peace or is my heart at war? Is there anxiety bubbling below the surface that is influencing my interactions with others? Am I operating out of genuine concern for the best possible outcome or am I just trying to win, no matter the cost? Healthy conflict is not blaming or accusatory but requires self-examination and self-control. Brian Cashman of the New York Yankees baseball team marveled at manager Joe Torre's ability to not let his own anxiousness bubble over to impact his players.

Torre, of course, wouldn't be half so effective in managing his employees or his boss if he weren't so effective in managing another person: himself. Though he admits to stomach-churning emotions during games--often chewing on Atomic Red-Hots to control stress and keep his mouth from getting dry – one wouldn't know it from his perpetually Sphinx-like expression. "Joe never panics, and you never see him berating a player," says Joe Girardi. "You never see him dropping his head in disgust." If anything, Torre manages countercyclically: As the situation grows more tense, he grows outwardly calmer, his mannerisms becoming even more deliberate. (Yankees general manager Brian Cashman calls these displays "calm bombs.") Conversely, when the Yankees are winning, Torre feels at liberty to turn up the heat on his players.[14]

Leaders who facilitate healthy conflict are able to drop calm bombs into the discussion in order for the team to make better decisions.

---

14 Useem, Jerry and Lisa Munoz. FORTUNE Magazine. http://archive.fortune.com/magazines/fortune/fortune_archive/2001/04/30/301967/index.htm. April 30, 2001.

Healthy Conflict Allows People to be Heard

Patrick Lencioni points out in his book, *Death By Meeting*, that so many meetings are boring because they lack conflict. You've seen it. Fewer people attend the meeting when it feels like everything has been decided before the meeting even takes place. Those meetings are just a series of reports on events everyone there had already attended. But let there be some controversy, and the meetings become standing room only!

As church people, we have a tendency to be nice. Someone says something in a meeting that we disagree with or have a problem with. We think to ourselves, *Am I the only one bothered by this? Should I say something?* We often end up remaining quiet until the meeting is over and then we discuss in the parking lot how upset we were by what was said. The meeting then doesn't really happen in the meeting itself. The real meeting ends up happening afterwards, when we are honest about our feelings and concerns. Healthy conflict brings those feelings and concerns into the actual meeting. Healthy conflict does not leave important concerns left unsaid.

Without healthy conflict, the loudest voices often rule the day. One simple device you can use to take a step toward healthy conflict in a meeting is to start a discussion with the entire group but then split people into small groups of two and three. Trust that where two or three are gathered, surely Christ is in the midst of them. Ask them to share their concerns in that smaller setting. People are more willing to share with one or two other people rather than risk being wrong or controversial in the large group. This technique also helps introverts to participate more fully.

Invite them to talk to their neighbor(s) for a minute about the topic at hand. Then have them all report to the group answering, "What concerns came up from that discussion? Was there something your neighbor said that could help us in this decision?" These small group discussions allow more perspectives to make their way into the room and cut down on the passive aggressive, post-meeting, parking lot problem solving. Moving people from being passive aggressive to pastorally assertive is a mark of healthy conflict. Pastoral assertiveness allows us to state clearly where we stand with a heart at peace. Passive aggressiveness seeks to wound from the shadows.

Orville and Wilbur Wright were their own small group and they didn't hold back because they wanted the best outcome.

During these months their "discussions" became as intense as they had ever been. Heated words flew, filling hours of their days and nights, often at the tops of their voices. "If you don't stop arguing, I'll leave home," a nearly hysterical Katharine cried out at one point. According to Charlie Taylor, they were never really mad at each other. One morning after one of their "hottest" exchanges, he had only just opened the shop at seven o'clock as usual when Orville came in saying he "guessed he'd been wrong and they ought to do it Will's way." Shortly after, Wilbur arrived to announce he had been thinking it over and "perhaps Orv was right." The point was, said Charlie, "When they were through...they knew where they were and could go ahead with the job." [15]

Healthy conflict allows us to say "I guess I was wrong." How willing are you to do that?

---

15 McCullough, *The Wright Brothers*, 89.

David Cummings suggests you can also change the tone of meetings in the long run and get people to take more risks if you ask the question, "Where have you failed since our last meeting? What did you learn from that failure?" When failure and risk-taking are honored, risk-taking multiplies. Healthy conflict allows us to share our failures and mistakes without risk of ridicule. One church staff began asking this question, "When did you last fail?" During the first couple of staff meetings it became a time of confession. Staff members would talk about mistakes they made and look for encouragement from the others gathered there. They seemed to be missing the point. Might we need to ask, "Where have you tried something that you couldn't have completed without help from beyond yourself? Where have you taken a grand risk for God and failed?" It is not much of a failure when the thing you were trying was not that important in the first place. Healthy conflict encourages experimentation, always growing, both yourself and your team. Healthy conflict stretches us for the older we get the more we need to stretch, but the less we do!

With a heart at peace, healthy conflict is not an end in itself but a means to live out the vision more fully with everyone on board. With a heart at war, people will engage in conflict for conflicts' sake.

Gutsy leaders take risks, including the risk to engage in conflict that can be misunderstood as hostility when the overall intention is better decision making and buy-in. Check your internal temperature. Are you engaging with a calm heart at peace or an angry heart at war?

When we end a conversation or are leaving one another's company, inevitably someone will say, "Take care." Years ago, Leonard Sweet taught the response, "Take risks."

Take the risk of engaging in healthy conflict. Take the risk of being wrong. Take the risk to be misunderstood. Take the risk to grow. Take the risk.

People will be more willing to agree to the outcome after more people have been heard.

Healthy Conflict Speaks the Truth in Love

In the South, you may hear someone say something about someone else followed by the phrase, "Well, bless their little heart." Or they might even say to you, "Bless your heart." It sounds like a kind word, but for those in the know, it is sometimes southern hospitality speak for "How could you be so stupid?"

> *"Bless your heart" is a phrase that is common in the Southern United States. The phrase has multiple meanings. It can be used as a sincere expression of sympathy or genuine concern. It can be used as a precursor to an insult to soften the blow. It is also sometimes used to mean "You are dumb or otherwise impaired, but you can't help it" by individuals who wish to "be sweet" and do not wish to "act ugly."* [16]

When I (Phil) arrived at the Stark United Methodist Church in Butts County, Georgia in the summer of 1992 one of the older gentlemen in the church took me on a tour of community, On our journey, he said, "Preacher, before you got here, we have had some highs and lows at this here church, but with you we want to find a happy mediocre." Too often churches settle for a happy mediocre rather than

---

16 "Bless your heart," Wikipedia, https://en.wikipedia.org/wiki/Bless_your_heart. Accessed May 16, 2019.

pushing through the difficult situations that can help us to grow as a church and as individuals. A few days later, preparations were underway for Vacation Bible School at that church. Being new, I asked how many children came to Vacation Bible School.

The answer was about thirty. We had more children than that in Sunday school on my first two Sunday mornings there. So, I suggested we cancel Vacation Bible School since it did not seem to be reaching the children of the community. You would have thought I had set off a roach bomb and not the calm bomb I had intended. The team who had always done VBS was offended if not downright incensed.

"What do you mean cancel VBS?" they exclaimed. Finally, one said, "What do you want from us?"

I said if we are going to put all this effort into creating a VBS, we ought to invite the children of the community. I asked what I thought was a simple question, "How do you advertise VBS?"

The answer: "We put it in the bulletin for a few weeks leading up to it."

I suggested they might want to advertise in the community. They had not done that in recent years. I went back to the idea of canceling. One member of the team said they had a sign they used to advertise their yard sale that could be repainted pretty easily to promote VBS. Another said she would create fliers and put them out at local businesses. Pretty soon word got out in the community that we were hosting VBS and everyone was welcome.

Over eighty children attended VBS that summer. One family who attended put a check for $1000 in the offering plate the Sunday afterward. I was notified of the gift and reached out to thank the family. They said, "We bring our daughters down here every summer from Ohio to see their grandmother. We never knew you were having VBS before but saw the sign and decided to attend. Our daughters can't stop talking about Jesus and singing the songs from VBS. We just wanted to say, 'Thank you.'" I asked if they wanted us to use the money for anything in particular and they said, "How about a better sign?"

The next month I was visiting with Kennon Callahan, a noted church consultant. I asked him for some advice on what the new church sign should look like. He started by asking where we were going to put the sign. I said, "In front of the church, of course. We would be replacing the old sign that was there because you can't change the message on it from week to week." He didn't say it but his look said, "Bless your heart." He then asked, "Why would you replace a perfectly good sign at the church? Why not find a place in your community with the large traffic counts and put a sign there that pointed toward the church?" Our ideas were in conflict but he presented his argument in such a direct and compelling way, I could not argue. We researched the traffic counts in our area and were surprised the crossroads down the road from the church had the most cars going by each month. A former church member owned property on one of the corners there and agreed to let us put up a sign with a large red arrow to point toward the church. Healthy conflict where the truth is told in love can grow us and our churches.

We have a bishop in North Georgia who speaks the truth in love. Bishop Sue Haupert-Johnson leads by calling for the church to become younger and more diverse just like our communities. The population outside of the church is younger and more diverse, so she unapologetically challenges our churches to reflect that. She does not run away from conflict because she knows healthy conflict can be transformative. In a meeting recently, I (Phil) was writing on a white board and each dry erase marker I picked up was out of ink. I went to place the pen back on the tray when the bishop blurted, "Throw that away. Why are you putting a marker back in place that is no longer working?" And yet we repeat this kind of behavior over and over. Healthy conflict speaks the truth in love, calling out the obvious that we have become accustomed to overlooking.

As Wilbur Wright so aptly put it, "No bird soars in a calm." Healthy conflict requires caution and close attention to advance preparation but you can be too cautious. Take the risk to engage in healthy conflict!

Equilibrium – balance – was exactly what riding a bicycle required and of that he and Orville knew a great deal. Well aware of how his father worried about his safety, Wilbur stressed that he did not intend to rise many feet from the ground, and on the chance that he was "upset," there was nothing but soft sand on which to land. He was there to learn, not to take chances for thrills. "The man who wishes to keep at the problem long enough to really learn anything positively must not take dangerous risks. Carelessness and overconfidence are usually more dangerous than deliberately accepted risks." As time would show, caution and close attention to all advance preparations were to be the rule for the brothers. They would take risks when necessary, but they were no daredevils out to perform stunts and they never would be.[17]

---

17 McCullough, *The Wright Brothers,* 48.

Fight Fair

Healthy conflict is assertive, stating its case, "Here I stand, I can do no other." Unhealthy conflict is aggressive, invading the space of others. **Healthy conflict is assertive.** In the South you might also speak of conflict by saying, "A little bit of his gravy gets all over my plate." Healthy conflict seeks to state its own position clearly. Aggressiveness seeks to impose its position on others.

Pastor Mike Schreiner, founding pastor of Morningstar in O'Fallon, Missouri shares that one of his toughest leadership lessons was around conflict. He talks about learning to run towards conflict. When he learned to lean into conflict, it changed everything. Running towards conflict allows us to care for the situation sooner. It also speaks to the healthiness of managing conflict. Conflict cannot be ignored. If it is ignored, it will only grow. But when conflict is managed with competent leadership, it is a healthy thing. Conflict is a not a bad thing. How it is managed determines the outcome. Healthy conflict happens when you manage yourself and your feelings during the conflict.

Gusty leaders engage in healthy conflict in order to move themselves and their organization forward.

CHAPTER FOUR

Healing Candor

Healing candor restores relationships. Healing candor allows us to admit the truth about ourselves. Healing candor can take the form of an apology. If you want to grow as a leader, you must engage in the often painful process of sharing and receiving healing candor.

Hurtful candor breaks relationships, sometimes even shattering them. Hurtful candor keeps us in bondage to our secrets and our resentment. Hurtful candor refuses to take responsibility for wrongdoing.

Gutsy leaders make a habit of healing candor.

Prayer for Cleansing and Pardon

Have mercy on me, O God,
  according to your steadfast love;
  according to your abundant mercy
    blot out my transgressions.
Wash me thoroughly from my iniquity,
  and cleanse me from my sin.

For I know my transgressions,

and my sin is ever before me.

Against you, you alone, have I sinned,

and done what is evil in your sight,

so that you are justified in your sentence

and blameless when you pass judgment.

Indeed, I was born guilty,

a sinner when my mother conceived me.

You desire truth in the inward being;

therefore teach me wisdom in my secret heart.

Purge me with hyssop, and I shall be clean;

wash me, and I shall be whiter than snow.

Let me hear joy and gladness;

let the bones that you have crushed rejoice.

Hide your face from my sins,

and blot out all my iniquities.

Create in me a clean heart, O God,

and put a new and right spirit within me.

Do not cast me away from your presence,

and do not take your holy spirit from me.

Restore to me the joy of your salvation,

and sustain in me a willing spirit.

Psalm 51:1-12 (NRSV)

Healing Candor Restores Relationships.

Have you ever played the game Paranoia? It's really quite simple. Every participant is given a clothespin or two. The object of the game is to put your clothespin(s) on someone else and to not end up with a clothespin on you. You play the game in a limited space. Playing for sixty seconds seems like an eternity. At the end of the game, people are surprised to find that someone has stuck a clothespin on them when they were so busy trying to put their clothespin on someone else. This simple game helps teams to reflect on questions like, "Do I have to watch my back with this team? Do others on this team have my back?" We played it once where one member of the team just stood in the center of the room and allowed everyone to put the clothespins on her, so others would not have to feel paranoid. Healing candor allows us to close the door on past wrongs, and move past paranoia into health and forgiveness.

I (Phil) had a church member who used to see me online back when AOL had instant messaging. She would share things with me that caused me to be alarmed and then immediately drop off-line so I could not respond. Finally, late one evening, frustrated by these interchanges, I called her on the phone right after she had dropped a bomb about people being upset with me at the church. She questioned why I called her so late at night. I told her she could not keep telling me things and then just exit the instant messenger on her computer. She didn't like it, but we came to an understanding. If she was going to share issues with me, I would always respond in a timely manner. I would try not to react (emotionally charged) but to respond (intellectually charged). She continued this pattern in other ways for quite some time. One day, just as I was about to preside at a funeral, she walked up to me at the funeral home and mentioned how the family was upset about the plans for the meal after the funeral. She started to walk away when I stopped her. She said, "I know you don't have time to talk about this now, the funeral is about to start." I told her they could wait. We needed to resolve this.

I told her I was not able to trust her intentions in telling me things the way she did. It was not the content of her issues, but the way and timing of presenting them. She heard my struggle and worked to share things without walking away. Our relationship deepened as we moved into new ways of interaction with healing candor. It also made me consider the times when I had dropped bombs on others like that. Much conflict could be avoided by simply asking the other person, "Is this a good time?" And if it is not a good time, set a time together to have a more fruitful discussion of the issue at hand.

I told her of another member of the church who would often share concerns with me about the church. I never worried when that other person shared issues with me, because I knew she always had the best interest of the church in mind. That parishioner taught me the difference between worry and concern. Worry was an irrational obsession with something I might not be able to change. Concern was my rational response and the first step toward finding a solution. I was thankful to always know that when she shared an issue with me, I was to be concerned but never worried. Healing candor alerts concern but does not lead to worry because the intent is truthfulness in love.

One of my colleagues was serving a growing church that had outgrown its choir loft. They were in the midst of rearranging the altar area and the furniture therein. A member of the church came up to him to say the furniture in the altar area must remain where it is. "It has always been there," she said. To which he replied, "Quite frankly ma'am, when Jesus comes back, he's not coming for the furniture." He reflected that it was fun to say, and true, but was not the right thing to say at the time. He engaged in candor but not the healing kind. Yet, sometimes humorous candor can have a role, moving the conversation forward and causing reflection without being hurtful.

I (Phil) was serving a church in a fast-growing area that was quite diverse. Unfortunately, the church itself was not very diverse. I told the church one Sunday, quoting Rob Bell, "If you don't like diversity, you won't like heaven!" There was nervous laughter. Then I told them, "If you don't like diversity, you probably aren't going." They did not think that was funny, although it is the gospel truth. We worked diligently to help that church reflect the diversity of that community.

One simple way we did that was to open the doors of the church to community meetings like homeowners associations. The church trustees initially wanted to charge outside groups but then began to understand it as evangelism. The church rolled out the red carpet for these groups by providing an excellent welcome and hospitality.

The groups were encouraged to meet in the sanctuary. That way, if and when they decided to return to the church, they had already made the journey from the parking lot to the pew. Someone from the church was there to welcome the group, tell them about the "facilities" and invite them to come back and join us on a Sunday am. We also reminded them it was a house of worship and then we added with humorous candor that we had been to heated homeowners' meetings that could benefit from the presence of God. The diverse growth of that church can be traced to the homeowners' meetings.

When one person from a neighborhood started attending the church, it had a multiplier effect.

Even with people we love and are closest too, we need to engage in healing candor. The Wright brothers were separated by the Atlantic Ocean and a lack of communication had led to misunderstanding. When people do not have information, they tend to fill in the gaps in ways that are not helpful nor healing. Wilbur had to write a letter of healing candor to his siblings in order for them to get back on track.

The morning of July 17, from his room at the Meurice, Wilbur wrote a long reply to Katharine setting straight for her and Orville the situation in Paris, how he was going about his part in it, his concern for them, how he had tried to spare them aggravation, and why they need not worry. It was noticeably candid and entirely confident in tone, and as revealing of his own estimate of himself as almost anything Wilbur ever wrote, his message being that he was the one on the scene in Paris, he was in command, knew what he was about, knew the people with whom he was dealing, and there was no call for those at home to get worked up. "In view of the fact that I have written, alone, three or four times as many letters home as I have received from all of you together," he began, "it is a little amusing to read your continual complaints that you get so few from me." In the two and a half months he had been away, he had received, on average, a letter a week from home, whereas he had been writing to them three to four times a week, except for a ten-day stretch when things were in such an unresolved state that there was nothing to report.[18]

---

18 McCullough, *The Wright Brothers*, 145.

Healing Candor Allows Us to Admit the Truth About Ourselves

When I (Phil) was serving the Lowell United Methodist Church, we had one member of the church who refused to sing certain hymns or say parts of the Apostle's Creed that he didn't agree with. I was impressed by his pursuit of integrity. One day, he called to ask if I could meet him over at the church that evening. I said I could, but then I worried for the next several hours about what he wanted to discuss. In years since, I have learned not to take on that anxiety but to ask, "What do you want to talk about so I can better prepare for our conversation?" Anxiety erupts from uncertainty. By discovering the topic of conversation, I could concentrate on the solution, rather than fretting over the subject matter. His words did not cause the worry but because I didn't have enough information, I had ramped up my concern into worry while I waited.

When we met that evening, we sat in the sanctuary. He looked at me and said, "I want to get baptized and join the church." I had the presence of mind to ask the Wesleyan question. "Have you ever been baptized before?" He said, "Of course! When I was growing up, I got baptized in the Baptist Church and joined the church." Before I could say that was great, you don't need to be baptized again, he went on. "Then I was at a Pentecostal Holiness revival and I felt moved by the Spirit and went down to the altar to be baptized." I tried to intervene again but he went on. "Then I married a woman who was a member of the Christian Church. So, I got baptized there and joined that church. I didn't do that when I married a Methodist. I wanted to be sure I was doing the right thing. So, I waited, I listened, and I studied. Now I want to get baptized and join The United Methodist Church."

69

This was my first assignment as a pastor. In fact, I was just a student pastor in my third year of seminary. I knew we did not re-baptize people so I hesitated in how to respond. Finally, after a prayerful moment, I felt nudged to calmly say, "Jimmy, maybe you don't need to be baptized again. Maybe you just need to change your life. Getting baptized again seems like you are asking God to redo God's part. Maybe it's time for you to redo your part. You don't have to get baptized again to join this church." Whew! I said it and then I waited. He shook his head and told me that he needed to think about it and pray about it. I said I understood and we prayed together.

He never mentioned getting baptized again but he did join the church, took a Disciple Bible Study Class, and then wanted to become a Certified Lay Speaker. Not long after that he expressed a call to the ministry and served rural churches as a local pastor for many years. Speaking the truth in love can be healing, but it is seldom easy.

When we watch the Great British Baking Show, we often cringe at the critiques offered by Paul Hollywood to the contestants. Some people would say, "He can just be so mean." Yet, for those who are most open to it, his candor is healing as he tells them the truth about themselves and challenges them to become better. I worked with one minister early on who was so gushingly complementary of everyone that you could not take a compliment from him seriously, because you had seen him go overboard with praise so many times when it was not merited. Leaders who want to grow are craving honest feedback. Healing candor gives us the fuel to grow and change. I (Phil) once submitted a Pentecost sermon to be critiqued by a pastor I worked with. I had put countless hours into it because I wanted it to be excellent and to impact the church for good. When he gave it back to me, it simply had scrawled on it, "This looks good." Healing candor can make us better if we are open to it. I still hear the echoes of the lines written on a paper I once wrote in seminary. In red letters the professor wrote, "I expected more of someone with your capability." That healing candor caused me to dig in to become a better student. When Paul Hollywood offers a handshake for an excellent bake, you know you have done something with excellence! And you strive to do it again! Contestants share that candid feedback on the Great British Baking Show pushes them to become better bakers.

Healing Candor Can Take the Form of an Apology

In raising a family, my wife and I have discovered some rules of thumb that make decision-making easier:

- You never regret going.
- You never regret taking the high road.

A wise member of the church in Grayson taught me that I needed to learn to be willing to apologize even when I didn't think I did anything wrong. He said in his business, he often apologized when things didn't go as planned, even when he had done everything in his power to make things go well. He said a willingness to apologize would make me a better leader.

You never regret apologizing for how your actions made another feel.

We had one family in that church who had a habit of getting mad and leaving the church for a period of time. It had become a pretty constant cycle over the years. They would get their feelings hurt and tell everyone they knew about how the church had wronged them. The wife of the couple also happened to be the best friend of the woman who would send an online message to me and then get off-line. They left the church while I was there over an incident with the music director. I took the advice of that fine leader and went to their home to apologize for what happened and for how they were hurt. They accepted my apology and came back to the church for awhile. A year or so later, an incident happened with the trustees. So, the family left the church and I made the same trek to their home to apologize for how the trustees had made them feel. It happened a third time but I can't even remember what the issue was. After this happened three times, her best friend took me aside and said, "I see the pattern now. You have always been so good about reaching out to them, but this really is about them and not our church. You don't have to do it anymore." What a moment of healing candor. She had recognized my faithfulness and gave them permission to leave without me having to chase them. That does not mean that you don't leave the ninety-nine to pursue the one, but rewarding bad behavior with more attention will not help you or your church grow.

One of our United Methodist Bishops has a habit of responding to email criticisms with the phrase, "You may be right."

In times of great struggle and disagreement, there is an even greater need to engage in healing candor after the conflict. Ron Greer, pastoral counselor at Peachtree Road UMC in Atlanta offers these suggestions for engaging in healing candor. What follows are his guidelines for relating one-to-one to people with whom they disagree:

1. **REMEMBER THAT THERE IS SO MUCH MORE THAT UNITES US THAN DIVIDES US**

   Our mutual high calling in the name of Christ continues to bring us together.

2. (As we engage in these conversations) **FOCUS ON RELATIONSHIP AND HEALING**

   If you came away feeling victorious, be respectful and humble.

   If you came away feeling defeated, be respectful and gracious.

3. **STAY CONNECTED WITH THE PERSON, THOUGH YOU DIFFER ON THE PERSPECTIVE**

   A difference in viewpoint in no way requires a breach in the relationship.

4. **GET TO KNOW THEIR STORIES**

   We assume if we know how another sided, we know who they are. We don't.

5. **LISTEN FOR THE TRUTH AND WISDOM IN EACH PERSPECTIVE**

   None of us have a corner on it, of course.

6. **BEGIN EACH CONVERSATION ON THIS TOPIC WITH LISTENING, ATTENTIVE LISTENING**

   Focused, intentional listening is truly a sacred silence

7. **CIVILITY IS THE LOW BAR - WE ASPIRE TO EMPATHY AND COMPASSION**

   Agape is a cornerstone of who we are as a Church. We aspire far higher than civility.

8. (Then when it's your turn) **SPEAK THE TRUTH IN LOVE**

   What we speak is the truth. How we speak it is with love.

9. IF THE TONE GETS ANGRY, LISTEN FOR THE HURT AND FEAR BENEATH THE ANGER

Listen for how they have been wounded. Listen for what frightens them.

10. IF THE CONVERSATION HEADS SOUTH, LOOK FIRST IN THE MIRROR

Are you seeking the truth or are you seeking to win?

Gutsy leaders are willing to apologize for how what they have done affects people, even when they can't apologize for their actions. Healing candor is not accusing or blaming. Wilbur Wright was not only healing in his speech, but even in his demeanor as evidenced in this recollection.

On Wilbur Wright

Her first impression was not altogether favorable, she admitted. "M. Wright appeared a bit too rough and rugged. His expression was fixed and terribly stern. But the moment he opened his lips to speak, the veil of severity vanished. His voice is warm, sympathetic and vibrating. There is a kindly look that imparts exceptional charm and refinement to his bright intelligent eyes... The frank honest way in which he looks straight in the eyes of the person to whom he speaks, and the firm grip of his wiry, muscular hand seem to give true insight into his character and temperament. He impressed me as one of the most remarkable men I have ever met.[19]

Healing candor leads in a frank, honest way. Gutsy leaders make a habit of healing candor after engaging in healthy conflict. Where might you need to follow up with healing candor today?

---

19 McCullough, *The Wright Brothers*, 205.

CHAPTER FIVE

Humbled Confidence

Demonstrating confidence is a positive and much needed leadership trait. Confident leaders are convicted to lead towards the mission and vision. They are surrounded with people who have faith, trust, credence, and belief in their leadership. People who work with confident leaders find the leader to be self-assured, poised, courageous, bold, and dependable.

But, here's the rub. Too many leaders are overly confident to the point of being arrogant. Arrogance is not an attractive or effective leadership trait. Arrogance leaves little room for God. Arrogance literally implies, "I have no questions."

There is a balance of having a healthy dose of confidence without being overly confident. We refer to this as humbled confidence. It is what Bishop Ken Carter refers to as a convicted humility. Humbled confidence is confidence which is self-effacing, unassuming, unpresuming, and respectful. Sometimes that convicted humility is earned through the mistakes made in times of overconfidence A humbled, confident leader knows who she/he is and who she/he is not. A humbled, confident leader is always learning while at the same being bold and courageous enough to be innovative. A leader learns after she/he has learned it all! Gutsy leaders exhibit humbled confidence. Like the apostle Paul stated in I Timothy:

> [12] *I am grateful to Christ Jesus our Lord, who has strengthened me, because he judged me faithful and appointed me to his service,* [13] *even though I was formerly a blasphemer, a persecutor, and a man of violence. But I received mercy because I had acted ignorantly in unbelief,* [14] *and the grace of our Lord overflowed for me with the faith and love that are in Christ Jesus.*
>
> I Timothy 1:12-14 (NRSV)

Be a Hero Maker

Heroes are celebrated for their courageous acts, special achievements, and noble character. Behind every hero is at least one hero maker. Hero makers live in the shadows, often nameless, but faithfully embracing the role of supporting character. They seek to make heroes who make heroes who make heroes. They invest in others to see the full potential of others released into others. I think of Barnabas, the hero maker to Paul and others. The scales had barely fallen from Paul's eyes before Barnabas had taken him to the apostles and vouched for him. Barnabas shifted from hero to becoming the mentor who creates heroes that ultimately become mentors (i.e., Paul to Timothy). [20]

Hero makers show up in all sorts of ways. It is the worship leader who raises up a musician or vocalist to be

---

20 Wilson, Todd. "Hero or Hero Maker: Which Will You Be?" Accessed May 14, 2019. Exponential.org. https://exponential.org/hero-heromaker/.

in the limelight, when the worship leader could have kept the light solely on him/herself. It is the pastor who gives the lay leader the credit for the collaborative action step the two of them created. It is the staff leader who gives the team all the glory for the event being pulled off without a hitch. I (Phil) recently congratulated a leader in our conference for completing a successful building project which was followed by a packed service of dedication and consecration. Without missing a beat, he replied, "Didn't the team just outdo themselves? I am so grateful for their work and creativity." It is the planting church who credits the newly birthed church with all the successes of the new launch. Hero makers do not need to receive the credit. Hero makers receive joy in equipping and sending others off to do the great things God created them to do. The hero maker has no need to take any credit for what God has done. The hero maker is humbled by God using her or him to lift others up.

Vulnerability

Humbled, confident leaders are vulnerable. They are not afraid to fail. They know that in being vulnerable to try new things, new faithful steps forward will be identified and successfully implemented. Being vulnerable means trusting completely in the possibilities. Vulnerability requires confidence, but if one is overly confident vulnerability can turn into recklessness. Vulnerability is knowing we don't have all the answers and are secure in knowing this. Knowing that being bold is required of being an effective leader even when one may fail leads us to humbled confidence with vulnerability. Having a healthy dose of vulnerability is an important attribute of a competent leader. A leader does not have to have all the answers, but is willing to be vulnerable to risk finding the answers.

Again, ponder the entrepreneurial leader who always asks his team at a staff meeting, "Tell us about the most recent time you failed." They inevitably start out by admitting mistakes they have made. This appears to be vulnerability but in fact they are usually not digging deep for their answers. He has to point out that making mistakes in our day-to-day work is not the same as trying something bold and then failing to achieve it. He is trying to push leaders to take gutsy risks that can pay great dividends for the team. When have you failed recently when trying something that stretched you beyond your comfort zone? When have you stretched to the point that you have become vulnerable to failure?

Integrity

A humbled, confident leader is full of integrity. Integrity is being trustworthy and demonstrating ethics, morality, and worthiness. Integrity is doing the right thing even when people are not watching. Integrity reflects having a moral compass. Most people desire to be seen as exhibiting integrity. But some do not have self-awareness around their own sense of having (or not) integrity. One simply does not know if you really have integrity until it is tested. There are three types of integrity: moral, mental, and physical. Take a moment to reflect. How would you rate yourself on integrity? Moral integrity? Mental integrity? Physical Integrity? What gaps did you identify, if any? What next steps might you want to take?

One of our colleagues continues to bring the conversation back to Jesus. He preaches and teaches about Jesus.

When people come to argue with him, he says to them, "It seems your argument is with Jesus about this and not with me."

After one of the many fatal shootings that have plagued our country, the gutsy leader at one of our churches preached about gun control. He was an avid hunter himself but made some concrete suggestions about ways to make guns, and the acquisition of guns, safer. The next day a livid church member came to complain about the sermon.

The pastor asked him, "What do you think Jesus would say about gun control?"

The incensed church member blurted, "I'd have to disagree with Jesus on that."

The pastor replied with the humbled confidence that comes from immersing yourself in scripture. "We try our best to represent Jesus and if you disagree with him on this issue, you will disagree with me, too, because I stand with Jesus."

Inclusive

Humbled, confident leaders are inclusive and make sure all on the team are heard. In a Forbes magazine article, "Five Leadership Lessons With A Gutsy Twist," this trait is covered in an article detailing the five leadership lessons from women.

> *The exclusive club is history. While in the past males often had their "private clubs," the gutsy women leaders of today know how to include everyone, regardless of gender, ethnicity, religion or economic background. This keen ability to include and to stand up for the right of everyone to be heard and considered is what separates those who live in fear from those who stand for freedom and justice.*[21]

21 Lafair, Sylvia. "Five Leadership Lessons with A Gutsy Twist." Forbes Woman. https://www.forbes.com/sites/womensmedia/2011/05/26/five-leadership-lessons-with-a-

As stated earlier, when meeting in a large group, some voices are silenced because they just happen to be introverts and are not willing to share their ideas in front of a large group. Others lack confidence in their ideas or suggestions and fail to share them with their neighbors. A wise mentor taught me to take time during meetings and seminars, to have people turn to one or two other people to discuss the item at hand. You will get a much richer flow of information when you invite people to talk to each other during the meeting. The things that are left unsaid can then be brought into the room during the meeting rather than after the meeting in the parking lot. One pastor remarked that he can tell the health of a church based on its parking lot emptying time. If the parking lot empties too quickly after worship, you might have a problem. If a parking lot does not empty quickly after a meeting, you might have a problem.

Celebration

Humbled, confident leaders celebrate with their team. Because humbled, confident leaders are hero makers, they are quick to lift up others' contributions and celebrate other's accomplishments. They are quick to shine the spotlight on others. Credit for accomplishments and goal attainment is given to the team. Celebration is key to taking the time to smell the roses and provide kudos to create a spirit of collaborative team work.

In the midst of a difficult week, Jesus took the time to celebrate the Passover with his disciples.

When it was time, he sat down, all the apostles with him, and said, "You've no idea how much I have looked forward to eating this Passover meal with you before I enter my time of suffering. It's the last one I'll eat until we all eat it together in the kingdom of God." Taking the cup, he blessed it, then said, "Take this and pass it among you. As for me, I'll not drink wine again until the kingdom of God arrives."

Taking bread, he blessed it, broke it, and gave it to them, saying, "This is my body, given for you. Eat it in my memory." He did the same with the cup after supper, saying, "This cup is the new covenant written in my blood, blood poured out for you.

Luke 22:14-20 (MSG)

Humility

Rev. Ken Carter is the President of the Council of Bishops for The United Methodist Church. He wrote the following in *Volume 1, 2019 General Conference Advanced Daily Christian Advocate.*

One of the core concepts in the final report of the Commission on a Way Forward is "convicted humility" (Daily Christian Advocate, p. 127). This concept is found in the Theological Framework for all three plans, and was a collaboration of members of the Committee on Faith and Order and the Commission on a Way Forward. Our conversation was guided by Greg Jones of Duke Divinity School and the statement was later affirmed by the commission.

A convicted humility is deeply scriptural. *Jesus matured in wisdom and in years, and in favor with God and people* (Luke 2:52, NRSV). *Now I know partially,* as Paul writes in 1

81

Corinthians 13:12, *but when I see God face-to-face, I will know completely.*

Why is this important? We are simply all on a journey in loving God and our neighbor, and none of us has arrived. We are all on a similar path of knowing God, and knowing the mind of God (Romans 11:34, NRSV), and knowing our brother or sister or enemy. Peter, after denying Jesus three times, grows into a humbled confident leader throughout the book of Acts.

I have not arrived at complete maturity or knowledge. I am not there yet. I believe God still has something (many things) to teach me.

Why is this important now? A convicted humility gives us a way of living with conscience, amidst others who see matters of faith, worship, and justice differently. We call this the church, the body of Christ, which is both one and diverse (1 Corinthians 12:14, NRSV).

Gutsy

Confident leaders are gutsy. They do not shy away from making the tough decisions. They are first to lead innovation. They are not afraid of failing. The leader who is both confident and humbled is able to effectively balance risk and reward. They also encourage those they work with to do the same.

Even Walmart has started to remind its people to be gutsy, giving team managers attitude cards to share with their co-workers with phrases like, *Be Bold, Be an Owner, Be Open,* and *Be Kind.*[22]

---

22 For more on this, visit https://www.andnowuknow.com/bloom/walmart-restructures-store-management-and-operations-Doug-McMillon-Drew-Holler/jordan-okumura/62861.

Humbled, confident leaders support innovation and risk-taking in their team. They are ready to be the safety net when those on their team fail, while also encouraging them to get up and try again. Great leaders are gutsy leaders who also encourage gutsiness in other leaders.

Humbled Confidence Recap

Humbled, confident leaders:

- Are Hero Makers

- Are Vulnerable

- Exhibit Integrity

- Celebrate Wins

- Practice Humility

- Are Gutsy Leaders.

Take a look at the attributes listed above. Where are your strengths on this list? Gaps? What is your next step in being a more humbled, confident leader?

Humbled confidence is the gift of experience.

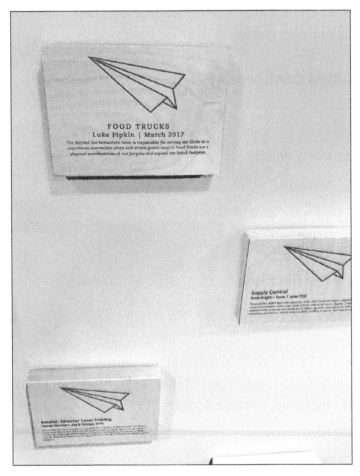

The principle of the Paper Airplane Award, according to Woody Faulk of Chick-fil-A's Innovation Center, is to celebrate accomplishments and failures.

CHAPTER SIX

Hope-filled Collaborations

God can do anything, you know—far more than
you could ever imagine or guess or request in your
wildest dreams! He does it not by pushing us around
but by working within us, his Spirit deeply and
gently within us.

Ephesians 3:20 (MSG)

Ministry is not a solo sport. We simply cannot go at it alone. Ministry is instead a team sport. It is meant to be done as a team full of people with diverse gifts, experiences, and thoughts. Even airplane pilots have co-pilots, sometimes engineers, and a team creating hospitality throughout the plane. Football, baseball, and basketball are all played with teams. Even in the solo sport of golf, the player has a caddy. Jesus had a team of twelve disciples.

So why do so many people in ministry try to go about ministry alone? In our experience, many pastors go about ministry alone for a variety of reasons. Those top reasons include not being equipped to build teams, a soloist attitude, and not being a collaborative partner. In this chapter, we will explore ways to overcome these common factors and others that keep leaders trapped in solo ministry. In addition, we will explore the benefits of being a hope-filled collaborative partner in ministry.

Teaming

The whole purpose of being a team is to come together to accomplish something more together than we could by ourselves. Coming together with multiple people provides the opportunity to bring together a variety of skills, gifts, experiences, and personalities. Different teams need different gifts from each of their team members. We must be intentional in assembling the team who will have the best chance of accomplishing the purpose together. Too often we allow the team to come together without purposeful and intentional planning. What skills are needed? What perspectives would be helpful? What are the needed skills for the team and the team's purpose? Too often we put together a team as though we are just looking for warm bodies to say "yes" to the invitation. It is as though we have a baseball player, a golfer, a tennis player, a football player, a bridge player, and a track runner coming together to try to play ice hockey. We sometimes simply do not have the right players on the team with the right skills and experiences. Yet, we still expect to win the ice hockey game! We are setting ourselves up for failure before we even begin.

Teams do not come together for the sake of coming together. In today's culture, people want to come together for a purpose, accomplish the purpose, and then disband. People are also looking for purpose and to make a difference for people. The difference they seek is a broad spectrum anywhere from local to global impact. Effective leaders can pull together teams that are purpose-driven and allow team members to use their gifts to truly made a difference in the world to one degree or another.

During a local church consult, Ken Callahan once said that too often when we call someone about a role in the church, we start by downplaying the importance of the work. "Now, we have called several other people and asked them to serve on the trustees and no one wanted to or was able to do it so we decided to ask you. You don't really have to do anything. We just need to put someone's name on the paper." People are not looking for more work, they are looking for meaningful work. Instead, he suggested that leaders ask people to live into their giftedness. He asked a young woman to remember middle school and the struggles of being a middle school girl. He then invited her to consider falling in love with a group of eighth grade girls, showing them the love of Christ. It is a great feeling when someone recognizes a gift we think or hope we have and asks us to use it to make a significant difference for Christ. Hopeful or hope-filled collaboration calls us to use our gifts for God's purposes together.

Collaborative Teaming

Let's take this to the next level. Both teamwork and collaboration involve a group of people working together to complete a shared goal. But there is indeed a key difference between the two. Teamwork pulls together the efforts of all the individuals. On the other hand, teams who are collaborative work toward the end goal collectively. The key difference between the two is that while teamwork combines the individual efforts of all team members to achieve a goal, people working collaboratively complete a project collec-

87

tively. Paul uses the word synergy in Romans 8, reminding us that all things work together for good.

Everything is permitted, but everything isn't beneficial. Everything is permitted, but everything doesn't build others up. No one should look out for their own advantage, but they should look out for each other.

I Corinthians 10:23-24 (CEB)

As Paul teaches us in the passage above, part of our Christian walk is to look out for one another. We should build one another up. Working in hope-filled collaborations helps us build one another up and look out for one another. When spiritual leaders work collaboratively with one another, they are working together towards fulfilling the mission of making disciples and living into the church's unique vision. When we collaborate with other like-minded people who are also on the intentional faith development pathway, things have a way of being purpose-driven. Anything outside the scope of the mission and vision will be dismissed. We become focused and purpose-driven through collaboration.

Add a Heap of Hope

But those who wait for the LORD shall renew their strength, they shall mount up with wings like eagles, they shall run and not be weary, they shall walk and not faint.

Isaiah 40:31 (NRSV)

Unfortunately, we have both been in church situations where hope has been lost. At best, apathy has set in. In

88

some of the worst cases, all hope is gone. How can we be the church and have no hope? How can we be followers of Jesus and have no hope? Isn't Jesus the hope of the world? So as Jesus followers, wouldn't we possess that same hope and want to offer it to others? Effective leaders are quick to offer hope to all. Leaders see the silver lining. Leaders see Jesus at work in all things. Leaders are the first to offer hope and are continuously reminding followers to be hope-filled, too.

We will often walk into struggling churches that are depressed. They cannot even imagine the next faithful step because they feel like nothing is going to work. Depression is not an easy thing to come out of, whether as a church or as an individual.

For these churches, so much has changed and all the things they have tried are not really working. They have moved along the grief process through anger, denial, and bargaining but have gotten stuck in depression. They can't see a way out of their struggles.

Being a hope-filled leader is not about offering words empty of belief. Hope-filled leaders truly believe there is always hope. They believe in the power of Jesus Christ to bring hope to the world. They are the "cup half-full" (and overflowing) people. In fact, they are always willing to say "Fill my Cup, Lord" no matter how much they have in their cup. Overall, they tend to see potential and possibility in everything.

Every day is a promise of God showing up in such amazing ways that we could never imagine on our own. We can't wait to see where and how God will move. Hope-filled leaders are able to offer that hope and vision to those around us.

Let's Put it All Together

Gutsy, effective leaders are hope-filled collaborative partners. These leaders sometimes come into this leadership trait naturally and instinctively. Other leaders must evolve into hope-filled collaborative partners. Wherever you are on the spectrum, this is a trait that must be fully embraced, learned, and practiced.

When church leaders are challenged to be better leaders, we often think about better leadership INSIDE the church. Yes, better leadership inside the church is always helpful. We are always about evolving into our best possible selves. But we sometimes forget about developing leadership for working OUTSIDE the church, too. Both inside and outside hope-filled collaborative leadership is required to be an effective and competent leader.

What does hope-filled collaborative leadership look like inside the church? There are many opportunities to offer hope-filled collaborative leadership inside the church. We will offer a few examples to provide some insights and get your mind thinking about all the opportunities to use this skill.

- Gather unlikely teammates (collaborative) together to dream about a brand-new ministry that would allow the church to live into God's preferred future for the church (hope-filled). Paint the picture (hope-filled) for the team of how the faithful works of this team could be an integral part of church's mission and vision.

- Work with your finance, trustee, and staff-parish relation-ships committee collectively (collaboration) to see how their work together can more fully align with the church's mission of making disciples of Jesus Christ for the trans-formation of the world (hope-filled).

What does hope-filled collaborative leadership look like outside the church? There are many opportunities to offer hope-filled collaborative leadership outside the church. We will offer a few examples to provide some insights and get your mind thinking about all the opportunities to use this skill.

- Gather laity from your church who have a shared desire to impact their community. For example, the group could have a shared concern for reading literacy at the local elementary school. Work with the school to match the church team with leaders at the school (collaborative) on possible solutions to improve the literacy level (hope-filled).

- Gather a team from your church who share a desire to feed the economically challenged people in the community who have food insecurities. Work with community leaders to find (collaborative) solutions to overcome these challenges (hope-filled).

Next Steps for Development

1. Check your go-to outlook. Are you the one who first points out the negative or the positive? Do you offer hope or criticism? If you are not sure, ask your family and close friends for some feedback.

2. Do you have a tendency to naturally build teams? Or are you more likely to pull together a team to work on it together? Watch for teaming opportunities.

3. Do you tend to go into team meetings with answers or questions? Leading with answers does not always promote collaboration. Leading with questions is more likely to create a collaborative culture.

Take a look at the steps above. Which step would you take to develop as a more gutsy leader? Hope-filled collaborators are a vital part of twenty-first century church leadership.

Part Two

Introduction

You have now been introduced to leading yourself and the traits and practices of spiritual leaders. Next is learning to lead others. In order to lead others, it is wise to have a process or pathway for equipping. We often have the best of intentions, but without intention and a process, the equipping and investing in others (like many best intentions) just does not happen. Days turn into months that turn into years. And before you know it, you have a generation or two of people in your congregation who have had little or no leadership preparation.

One must become intentional in changing behaviors in order for the new practice to become habit and maybe even become second nature. For a process to be life-giving and life-changing, it must also be intentional. Leaders do not develop just because we want leaders developed. Leaders develop because we have an intentional, step-by-step process to ensure the best possible outcome.

As we discuss developing and launching leaders in the church, who are we referencing? Leaders in your church include staff, current leaders, future leaders, the next generation of leaders, clergy, and laity. We are often trying to backtrack and invest in leaders who we are asking to step up to the leadership plate today. Leaders include both paid and unpaid staff. We often refer to unpaid staff as those who are leading ministry areas but not on payroll. Not all clergy have encountered leadership equipping as part of their training, either. We often assume clergy have been developed as leaders, but in our experience, this is just not the case by and large.

With this intentional leadership development process, we are hoping to introduce a culture of leadership development. Of course, you will need to equip your current leaders if you have not done so already. Yet at the same time, you will want to consider who is the next set of leaders for next year and the year after. How are you equipping children, youth, and young adults for leadership?

Five Levels of Leadership Development

As you take off on this journey of launching leaders, you will encounter five different levels of leadership development. This will be the development process within each session that in turn shifts the way of being and doing life.

Five Levels of Leadership Development:

Ponder	Check you Gauges
Provoke	Start your Engines
Process	Take Off
Probe	Climbing and Soaring
Practice	Taxi

In Addition to the Five Levels:

Potential Resources	Flight Simulators

Each session starts with prayer and play, then leadership development at the ponder level. This is where we first

94

examine the subject and introduce ideas and concepts. As you can see as one progresses from the pondering stage to the provoke and process stages, we bring power to the subject and begin to explore limiting beliefs and assumptions. At the process level, we begin to fly and practice our new leadership habit. When practice begins, participants are starting to soar and own their new leadership habit. In between sessions, launching leader participants will be able to actively practice their development by exploring and using new resources to hone and practice their skills.

As we begin to consider take-aways and action steps, we will monitor our development and ideas by considering this question: Is this our goal, a good idea, or is this a Godly idea? This helps keep our leadership spiritually grounded and in alignment with God's preferred future instead of our own perceptions. This is a great gut-check to next steps. As Mike Selleck, retired pastor from North Georgia states, "A good idea comes out of someone's head, a Godly idea has leaders and servants attached so we know it is God's time for the work and not just our desire."

The Invitation

Here are some things to consider when deciding who to invite into the Launching Leaders process. First and foremost, if you have already had individuals in leadership positions, start with them to provide a shared language. Next, begin to discern who might be the next set of individuals who will need to be launched into new or greater leadership roles. This is your second group. Then, consider the types of individuals needed to most faithfully fulfill the mission and vision of your congregation. These could be new people in the faith, those who are leading in the secular world but not the church, and/or those who have been sitting on the sidelines because they feel ill-equipped to lead, but could and would lead beautifully if given the chance and fully equipped and invested in. Finally, do not forget about your youth and young adults. Invest in them early and often. You might even consider how to do this with young people outside the church!

Tom Davis, pastor of Roswell UMC teaches the four C's of hiring, but the characteristics are also true of finding and developing leaders. He posits that you look first for Character. You cannot put character into people if it is not there. Next, you look for Chemistry with the team. Then, you look for Competence, which, for most tasks within the church, can be developed. Finally, you look for Courage.

Character asks, "Who am I?"

Chemistry asks, "Who are we?"

Competence asks, "Can I do the job?"

Courage asks, "Will I do the job?"

As church people, we often look for people with secular experience and training. For example, when looking for people to serve on the finance committee, we often find ourselves asking people with banking or financial training and expertise. Or we are looking for people in the building trades to serve on the trustee committee. While their experience is helpful, we can hire that kind of expertise anywhere. What is more important than anything when it comes to spiritual leadership is a spiritual maturity. We often put in people who are spiritually immature for the sake of their secular expertise. The people who are making decisions on behalf of leading the church in its mission and vision should be the most spiritually mature people. People invited into leadership should be well into the intentional faith development process and living out their vows of prayers, presence, gifts, service, and witness. Take your spiritually mature people and pour into them to further develop them as leaders. Then, let these spiritually mature leaders take flight. It will be a beautiful thing!

Orville & Wilbur Wright

We most often associate the Wright brothers with the invention of the airplane. But we often miss the interesting portion of their story where it all began. The Wright brothers began their love of ingenuity and invention building bicycles. Because of this beginning curiosity in transportation and making things move, they were naturally curious about other modes of transportation and pushing the innovation envelope.[23]

In the earliest flying machine inventions, you will notice a direct connection to their experience in building bicycles. In essence, the Wright brothers were trying to invent a flying bicycle! They learned that you can't balance a bike that is not in motion. The same held true for airplanes. Both of these forms of transportation require balance. Likewise, leadership requires balance. Making decisions in leadership requires being in motion and balance.

In our *Launching Leaders* sessions, we will explore the life of the Wright brothers and how their experiences and opportunities in their growing up years were instrumental in setting them up as innovators in adulthood. We will also

---

23 "From Bike to Flight." Smithsonian National Air and Space Museum. https://airandspace.si.edu/ exhibitions/wright-brothers/online/who/1895/biketoflight.cfm. Accessed May 14, 2019.

tie in their own leadership development into the launching leadership development process

Biblical Leadership

Besides the leadership lessons learned with the Wright brothers, there will also be two biblical underpinnings in each session; an Old Testament and New Testament story indicative of the leadership trait the session is exploring. These stories will ground each spiritual habit and leadership quality biblically.

Order is Important

Each session will flow with the same format. The flow and order are critical and specially ordered for the best possible experience, outcome, and development. Please follow the order provided. Make sure to spend plenty of time in conversation. Invite everyone to participate in the conversation. Everyone's input and perspectives will be important to the conversation and richness of the experience.

Launching Leaders

Once you have completed Part One of this resource, you are ready to begin launching leaders using the resources found in Part Two. Review the information in the Part Two Orientation. As a best practice, please follow the invitation guidelines and gather your first Launching Leaders group. Once the group is selected, gather them for a time of orientation, covenant, and preparation for the Launching Leaders' six sessions. Let's get started with ground school so we can launch leaders into flight!

PART TWO
Orientation
Ground School

*This section is to be read by the leader of
the Launching Leaders class.*

*If I speak with human eloquence and angelic ecstasy
but don't love, I'm nothing but the creaking of a
rusty gate. If I speak God's Word with power, revealing all his mysteries and making everything plain
as day, and if I have faith that says to a mountain,
"Jump," and it jumps, but I don't love, I'm nothing.
If I give everything I own to the poor and even go to
the stake to be burned as a martyr, but I don't love,
I've gotten nowhere. So, no matter what I say, what I
believe, and what I do, I'm bankrupt without love.*

Love never gives up.

Love cares more for others than for self.

Love doesn't want what it doesn't have.

Love doesn't strut,

Doesn't have a swelled head,

Doesn't force itself on others,

Isn't always "me first,"

Doesn't fly off the handle,

Doesn't keep score of the sins of others,

Doesn't revel when others grovel,

Takes pleasure in the flowering of truth,

Puts up with anything,

Trusts God always,

Always looks for the best,

Never looks back,

But keeps going to the end.

Love never dies. Inspired speech will be over some day; praying in tongues will end; understanding will reach its limit. We know only a portion of the truth, and what we say about God is always incomplete. But when the Complete arrives, our incompletes will be canceled.

When I was an infant at my mother's breast, I gurgled and cooed like any infant. When I grew up, I left those infant ways for good. We don't yet see things clearly. We're squinting in a fog, peering through a mist. But it won't be long before the weather clears and the sun shines bright! We'll see it all then, see it all as clearly as God sees us, knowing him directly just as he knows us! But for right now, until that completeness, we have three things to do to lead us toward that consummation: Trust steadily in God, hope unswervingly, love extravagantly. And the best of the three is love.

I Corinthians 13 (MSG)

Before a new pilot is allowed to fly a plane, the pilot must first complete ground school. This is a time of learning to understand safety, instrumentation, and to gain overall knowledge for flying an airplane. A pilot does not start out flying a jet, but must first start in ground school, then fly with an instructor in a single engine plane and master it before going onto twin engine, small jets, and then commercial jets. We sometimes throw people into leadership asking them to lead like a commercial pilot when they have not yet flown a single engine plane, let alone been to ground school.

This section helps you take people through ground school

before climbing into the cockpit to fly. There is then a time of flying with an instructor before someone finally flies solo. Continuous and more in-depth training is needed before leaders are able to lead at the metaphorical level of jet pilots. In other words, this section is an intentional leadership development process. Processes are continuous. There is no stopping or ending point. We must continuously pour into leaders with resourcing and equipping to help our leaders become the best they can be and stay relevant and competent in their leadership. Not only is this beneficial for the church, but it benefits the individual personally and professionally.

The Importance of Play in the Wright Brother Home

At home, the enjoyment of Lorin's children coming in and out grew only greater for both Wilbur and Orville. Their niece Ivonette would say of Orville in particular that he never seemed to tire of playing with them, and that if he ran out of games, he would make candy for them. Wilbur, too, would amuse them in equally wholehearted fashion, though not for long. "If we happened to be sitting on his lap, he would straighten out his long legs and we would slide off. That was a signal to us to find something else to do. When we were old enough to get toys, Uncle Orv and Uncle Will had a habit of playing with them until they were broken, then repair them so that they were better than when they were bought.[24]

We, too, believe play is an important part of learning. Each session will include a time for play.

---

24 McCullough, *The Wright Brothers*, 376-381.

Paper Airplane

Each lesson will involve an activity with a paper airplane. The purpose of the activity is to promote creativity, tie the lesson of leadership into the flying metaphor, add a bit of a competitive nature, and to play together as a team. Come prepared to each lesson with paper for airplane construction. You may even want to add some other elements as you lead individuals through the lessons such as weights, markers, or other types of paper. Have fun with it. Play!

DiSC

As part of leadership development, we highly recommend each launching leader participant take the DiSC assessment. This assessment helps a person better understand their communication and leadership style and how she/he interacts with other leadership styles. There is no one "better" leadership type – just different. It is extremely important to know our leadership tendencies, to be more self-aware in order to become the most well-informed leader. Self-awareness is a critical leadership trait for effective leadership. DiSC helps the leaders and team members to become more aware of how they process information.

There are four unique leadership types.

DiSC Descriptors	Primary Tendencies
D=Dominance	Direct/Tell
i=Influencer	Persuade
S=Steady	Consult/Listen
C=Conscientious	Delegate/Systematize

Here is a link to a free DiSC assessment:

https://www.123test.com/disc-personality-test/

During Orientation, help each launching leader participant unpack their own assessment. Then spend some time on how the different types of leaders interact with one another. Indicate the primary drivers, communication styles, blind spots, and gaps for each. You might want to bring in someone who is certified in DiSC assessments to assist each participant in their individual assessment unpacking. They might also help lead the discussion for the group to help identify how the different leadership types in the room affect the dynamics of the conversation and how they work together.

You may like to substitute or add other leadership assessments. If you choose to do so, make sure the assessments are helping with leadership indicators and not just personality types. While learning about personalities is helpful, assessing leadership indicators will be most helpful since this process is about developing leaders. I (Kay) find StrengthsFinder to also be a very helpful assessment for leaders to know their strengths. The idea of StrengthsFinder is to build on strengths rather than the traditional way of addressing and shoring up one's gaps.

We have shared two tools we use with leaders, but you might have some others. The most important thing to understand is not necessarily the specific assessment chosen, but that individuals are most often not fully aware of their own leadership tendencies, recognizing the various styles in other people, and learning how to work best with the different leadership styles.

Habit Intro

In order to be the best version of ourselves, we most often find the need to continuously grow and adapt. We recurrently catch ourselves stuck in old habits that do not particularly support the best versions of ourselves. Many times those habits are hard to break. Growing and developing as a leader causes us to routinely and continuously self-evaluate. As a spiritual leader, our habits (or leadership practices) must coincide with our spiritual practices. Below you will find how spiritual and leadership practices (in particular the United Methodist membership vows) tie into one another in this process and in a life well-lived.

Spiritual Practices	Leadership Practices
1. Presence/Worship	Helpful Communication
2. Prayer & Study	Holy Conversation
3. Witness	Healthy Conflict
4. Gifts	Healing Candor
5. Service	Humbled Confidence
6. Spiritual Friendship	Hope-filled Collaboration
7. Accountability	Coaching

During each session together, *Launching Leaders* will explore how the leadership and spiritual traits tie in together. Because good practices first come with breaking old (sometimes ineffective and unhealthy) habits, a new spiritual practice is introduced each session along with the leadership practice. This gives each participant a chance to slowly develop good spiritual and leadership practices as they live into this process overall.

As each launching leader participant encounters the next six sessions, help them do more than learn the words. Come to the table to explore the real meaning of the words and how these traits might develop us as spiritual leaders. Take time to explore how the lessons within the words would be lived out in a shift in how each participant would go about life. Leadership and spiritual development are not only about knowing, but also about a different way of being because of the new knowing. Help participants dive into these shifts each session. This is where real transformation and growth will occur.

To help explore the application of these habits or practices, we will expect you to ask these questions of your participants at the end of each session. Below are examples of questions when you are exploring the spiritual practice of worshiping, being present with God.

- How am I different because of this week's spiritual practices?
- How am I growing because of my spiritual practice?
- How am I maturing as a disciple because of my spiritual practice?
- How am I inspired to be more because of this spiritual practice?

During this process, the pastor and laity leader are co-pilots. This is not about the pastor taking leaders or the congregation on a ride in the airplane. This is not about the pastor being the flight captain. Instead, this process is about the pastor developing alongside the leaders. Remember, the flight instructor does not sit in the captain seat. The student sits in the captain's seat!

Depending on the individual circumstances in your church, you may find that there is a lay person who would/ could lead this process. This is perfectly fine. In The United Methodist Church, there is a Nominations and Lay Leadership Development Committee. By polity, the pastor is chair of this committee. In our experience, most of the time this committee does the work of nominations and calls it a day.

Unfortunately, the leadership development part of the work of this committee goes by the wayside. The whole process could be led by someone from this committee, a solid leader already leading in the church, or the pastor. The right person leading is more important than the position that person holds.

Session Flow

Each session will have the same flow. Take some time to familiarize yourself with the elements, flow, and time allotment for each. You will notice there are two-time frames listed. We are offering two different session experiences. We refer to one as the Instant Pot version that lasts ninety minutes.

The other session experience is the Crock-Pot version which allows longer, more tender processing times and insights lasting up to two and a half hours. The longer time is optimal, but not always possible. Sometimes you just need something to move ahead faster.

Longer periods of time allow people to slow down more and be able to dive deeper into the lessons and more important the intended growth. Shorter sessions still move people through the lessons, but the learnings may tend to be more technical.

In considering the length your group will invest in this leadership development process, consider the opportunity cost. In other words, it may need a deeper investment upfront, but the payoff will be many times over. You may also be able to do the Instant Pot version if participants are willing to do more outside work on their own.

Activity	Time Allotment	Description
Pray	5/5	All take turns
Play	10/10	Paper airplane activities
Ponder	20/30	Prayer & Scripture from Old & New Testament (Feeling)
Provoke	25/45	Leadership Development - hard and heart questions (Feel & Think)
Process	15/30	Take-aways and next steps (Behavior)
Probe	10/20	Goals vs Godly Work
Practice	5/10	Spiritual & Leadership Habits (Differences Habits Make, Action Steps)
90/150		

Potential Resources

At the end of each session, you will find a listing with potential resources to use and/or perhaps dive deeper into topics, growth, and understanding. These can include both *pre-* and *post-* work including such things as books, movies, podcasts, and TED talks.

Getting Started and Ending Well

As a best practice, set expectations up front such as regular attendance, being fully engaged, full participation and commitment, completing the action steps, etc.

After the *Launching Leaders* sessions, you will be guided in a wrap up to launch your leaders into flight. This is a critical step in the process, so do not overlook this opportunity to celebrate and release participants into leadership flight.

Note to Leaders – Be sure to preview the videos for each session before showing them to the class in order to familiarize yourself with the content and be sure the links are working properly. Even Gutsy leaders don't like surprises that detract from the content of a session.

PART TWO
Session One
Helpful Communications

Leaders Who Communicate Helpfully Give Clear Direction Based on God-given Vision. Worship provides a venue for vision casting.

Prayer – Begin each session with prayer.   5/5 Minutes

Each day this week repeat this prayer:

> *God of Vision and Power,*
>
> *Open our eyes to see more clearly the direction in which You are calling us to go.*
>
> *Help us to write Your vision plainly so it becomes a part of us.*
>
> *May we be able to share Your vision without hesitation.*
>
> *Amen.*

Play   10/10 Minutes

Each person will need two pieces of plain paper. Instruct each person to take a piece of paper and make a paper airplane in their favorite style. Do not show your plane to anyone else. When you have finished your plane, pair up with another person. Describe your plane to them without allowing them to see it. Stand back to back and instruct them on the steps to create an exact replica of your plane. Then have them do the same for you. Compare the plane you created to the plane your partner created based on your instructions. How different are they? What could have been more helpful in your communicating your vision?

Ponder 20/30 Minutes

Read Exodus 3 and 4.

Take off your shoes before you start.

How does the act of reading with your shoes off affect your reading, interpretation, and understanding?

Discuss your discoveries from the text.

Ponder God's vision for your work. Choose some part of your life to consider: your family, your church work, your vocation. What one thing, if you did it with excellence, would most improve your personal life? What one thing, if you did it with excellence, would most improve your work life? Since what you answered it true, then why aren't you doing it?

Where have you let someone else's urgency dictate your actions?

Write a short, clear vision for your work. Keep it to the length of an elevator speech. An elevator speech is a short talk you are ready to give on a moment's notice when you find yourself in an elevator for a few floors with someone who needs to hear your vision. It requires you to get to the point and pitch your idea quickly and succinctly. There is a new church start pastor in Georgia at The Nett UMC, Rodrigo Cruz, who is always ready to state his vision. "We want to create a church that looks like our schools, that reflects on earth the diversity that is in heaven."

Read 1 Corinthians 1

Ask yourself:

- If I were to write a letter to my team, what would I need to say this week?

- If your team wrote back what would I need to hear?

- How does Paul's Vision for the Church come through in these words?

- When have you received helpful communication that helped you to stay centered?

Provoke   25/45 Minutes

Watch the Backward Bike video again:

https://ed.ted.com/featured/bf2mRAfC#watch

Key Points from the Video to discuss with the group:

1. Knowledge does not equal understanding. As you consider God's vision for your work, where do the people on your team have knowledge but not full understanding?

2. Neuroplasticity is the brain's ability to reorganize itself by forming new neural connections throughout life. Are there places where your brain might need to be retrained to live into a new vision?

Soren Kierkegaard challenged people to ask the question, "Who is the audience for worship?"

Fill in the chart below. Use these three possible answers on both sides:

The People • Pastor and Worship Team • God

In Practice	Roles in Worship	Ideally
	Audience	
	Actor(s)	
	Prompters	

The ideal answer is that God is the audience for worship. Yet in practice, most people think they are the audience for worship which is performed for their pleasure by a pastor and worship team or choir. If you don't agree, just listen to people after worship. There is a tendency to evaluate the worship service, from the preaching to the music to the lighting and temperature of the space. It is as though worship is for us, the participants, and not a sacrifice of praise offered to the creator of the universe. If we are the audience, then we ask, "Were we pleased with the service?" If we acknowledge that God is the audience, we must ask, "Was God pleased with what we offered to God today?" How would your attitude about worship change if you took seriously that it was your offering to God, and the hope is that God would be pleased with your offering? Below is the chart properly completed based on Kierkegaard's work.

In Practice	Roles in Worship	Ideally
The People	Audience	God
Pastor & Worship Team	Actor(s)	The People
God	Prompters	Pastor & Worship Team

Gil Rendle put it this way, "It as though we have confused purpose with preference." We are fighting about our preferences, so that we will be pleased rather than asking will God be pleased by the words of our mouths, the meditations of our hearts, and the actions we take on a daily basis. This exercise can help people to retrain their brains in how they thought about worship.

Helpful communication starts by asking the right question, "Will God be pleased?"

Immediately people push back, "Who are we to know the mind of God?"

I think we can say readily we know things in our lives that do not please God. But we might not be certain of what we are doing that is pleasing to God.

Process   15/30 Minutes

What realizations did you have in the exercise about worship personally? Congregationally?

Where do you see the tension between pleasing God and pleasing those in your congregation?

What message is being shared with the church overall, versus what message would you want to be shared?

What is a faithful step in improving the communication in worship? Beyond worship, what is your next step to be a more helpful communicator?

Probe   10/20 Minutes

Reflect on your next steps above. Are these baby steps or God-sized steps in faith? In becoming a more mature spiritual leader, in what ways do you want to be a better communicator and vision-caster a year from now? Are you dreaming God-sized dreams? Do you inspire others to do the same?

Discuss these questions with a partner:

- How will further developing spiritual disciplines help your faith walk?

- What challenges might you encounter in this development?

- How will you overcome these challenges?

- Who will you partner with in this journey for encouragement and accountability?

Practice   5/10 Minutes

To become a better and more mature spiritual leader, we must adopt spiritual habits to propel our growth. Each session will remind ourselves of the spiritual habits - taking one at a time and building one onto another until we are practicing all the spiritual practices. We start by regularly attending worship every week. Listen for God's helpful communication to you through the worship service. Where did you hear God most clearly? Ask yourself, "Was God pleased with the worship I offered today?" How will what you heard or learned in worship affect your life in the coming week and thereafter? Take notes during worship this week and remember to pray the prayer at the beginning of this lesson at the start of each day.

Potential Resources

Books:

Building a Story Brand by Donald Miller
Power of Vision by George Barna
Lead Like Jesus by Ken Blanchard

TED Talks:

TEDx Talks. "Power of a Vision: Brad Wolgamott at TEDx-Bountiful"

https://www.youtube.com/watch?v=66DXqosfZSQ. January 28, 2012.

Session Two

Holy Conversation

Leaders who engage in holy conversation listen for God in prayer and discussions.

Holy conversation builds vulnerability-based trust. Holy conversation moves us beyond our wants and needs to what might please God.

Prayer – Begin each session with prayer.   5/5 Minutes

God who speaks creation into being,

Invite us into the conversations you are having with the people of this world.

Help us to listen for your voice in others even when we struggle with their words.

Help us to listen to what is being said and listen to what is not said.

Speak to us again and again so that we can truly hear.

Here I am, Lord. Is it I, Lord? I have heard you calling in the night.

I will go, Lord, where you lead me.

I will hold your people in my heart. Amen.

117

Process Last Week's Lesson/Experience.

How was worship different for you? What did you notice? Where did you hear helpful communication this week?

Play   10/10 Minutes

Divide into pairs or small teams. Each team will receive three pieces of paper, to be used to create paper airplanes – one for each round. Fly the airplane after each round and log the distance traveled for each build.

Everyone must participate in each round. The first round of paper airplane building will be done without speaking – only using hand gestures. The second round will be built without speaking, but the team can mouth words to each other. The third round can be completed with all kinds of communication possible. You have sixty seconds for each round.

Compare the outcomes of the three rounds. Which design flew the furthest? Which round had the most collaboration? Which round was most frustrating? What did you learn from this exercise?

Ponder   20/30 Minutes

Read Exodus 6.

Where have you seen God at work in your history and in the history of your family? How about in the history of the church? Where do you think God is hearing groaning today in the world? In your community? In your work? In your family? In your church? In you?

Ponder the times in your life you feel like God has spoken to you. Write down one incident and share it with someone. Ask another person if they have ever had a time they felt like God had spoken to them. Did they listen? What was the result of that holy conversation? Reading verses 28-30, what might be holding you back from serving more fully? Do you have an insecurity that keeps you from being your best?

Read I Corinthians 2.

Reread verses 3 & 5. Where have you heard holy conversation, conversation that seemed to move beyond human wisdom?

Recall a time when you feel like you had just the right words to say? Where did those words come from? Did you experience those words as a gift from the Holy Spirit, allowing you to engage in holy conversation? Recall a time when someone spoke just the right words to you. What impact have those words had on your life to this point? What does it mean for you to "have the mind of Christ?" Where have you seen yourself mature in wisdom? Share an example with a friend or colleague. How does the gathered faith community offer wisdom? How does having the mind of Christ offer checks and balances to your conversations?

Provoke 25/35 Minutes

Watch this Heineken Ad:

Aaron Whittier: "Worlds Apart Open Your World1." *Heineken World.*

https://www.youtube.com/watch?v=dKggA9k8DKw.
Accessed May 15, 2019.

Discuss how you might have responded? What made these conversations possible? Share your reactions.

Pair up with another person in your group. In three sentences or less, share your personal core values. Were any of your attributes challenged by the Heineken Ad?

Next, shorten your stated personal core values to two sentences or several bullet points. Do your core values have an imperative quality that calls you to something more?

Try once again to articulate your core values in one concise sentence. Finally, share your story in six words or less (i.e. for sale, baby shoes, never worn).

What are your inherent biases?

Process   15/30 Minutes

What would you need to do in order to be more vulnerable and open to sharing the real "who of you? "What is a gap in your development of being the best version of a spiritual leader you can be: a truth teller with love and grace? What step would be needed to close this gap?

Probe   10/20 Minutes

Is the action step identified above a goal or is it Godly work to be done? Articulate your answer to clarify turning any goals into Godly work. How do you differentiate between Goals and Godly work?

Discuss these questions with a partner:

- How am I different because of worship?

- How am I growing because of my worship encounters?

- How am I maturing as a disciple because of my worship practices?

- How am I inspired to be more because of worship experiences?

Practice   5/10 Minutes

For further development as a gutsy spiritual leader, we need to expand our development for both spiritual habits and leadership habits. The spiritual habits we will be working on this week are daily prayer and Bible study. This is important so that you might have the mind of Christ to start the day. What is your current daily habit? What will you need to do differently in order to grow in your daily spiritual habit as a spiritual leader?

For further leadership development, practice having holy conversations. If you are new to having holy conversations, start practicing in safe places with loved ones. Then, progress to your workplace (if applicable) and then onto service teams in the church. Share with your leadership teammates your progression in this area.

How are you doing in practicing presence and worship, the other spiritual habits of a spiritual leader from last session?

Potential Resources

Books:

Crucial Conversations by Kelly Patterson, Al Switzer, Joseph Grenny and Ron McMillan.

The Emotionally Healthy Church by Peter Scazzero

Movies:

Places in the Heart

Where the Heart Is

Podcasts:

Episode 3: "The Kaleidoscope Effect: What Emerging Generations Seek in Leaders featuring Scott Chrostek."
Church Leadership.com.
https://www.churchleadership.com/podcast/kaleidoscope-effect-emerging-generations-seek-leaders-featuring-scott-chrostek/?id=lit-top20181226. Accessed May 15, 2019.

PART TWO

Session Three

Healthy Conflict

Conflict that is healthy is rooted in trust. Healthy conflict challenges us to grow and change. Healthy conflict isn't mean-spirited. Conflict is nothing more than the pursuit of truth or the best possible answer.

"Conflict without trust is just politics."

Patrick Lencioni

"No bird soars in a calm."

Wilbur Wright

Prayer   5/5 Minutes

God who doesn't shy away from conflict with the evils of this world,

Help us to stand up for what is right and just,

to engage in conflict over that which matters to you.

Amen.

Ponder   20/30 Minutes

Read Exodus 18.
Identify the steps that were taken before Jethro starts the healthy conflict conversation in verse 14. Where might you need to have a healthy conflict conversation?

Read I Corinthians 3.

How are you growing? Ken Willard offers the image of a church that just keeps adding high chairs rather than growing disciples that can feed themselves. What would a building inspection find in the house of your faith?

Provoke   25/45 Minutes

Watch and Discuss
Video: Shloul, Muhammad. Patrick Lencioni's "Fear of Conflict." YouTube.com.
https://www.youtube.com/watch?v=u4Pi7dbdTiQ. April 7, 2015.

The Wright brothers fought openly and vehemently about the best ways to go about their work. In fact, after a day of arguing one position, they would sleep on it and wake up the next day arguing the others position. Teams that did not have that kind of trust left things unsaid. Thus, they did not make the same progress toward flight that the Wright brothers were able to do.

Recall a time when you were involved in a situation where something was left unsaid. Was the situation later resolved? If so, how was it resolved? If not, what would need to be said or done to resolve the situation? Share your experience and the resolution with a partner.

If you did the DiSC assessment in session 1, discuss how your communication style impacts how you deal with conflict. If you did not do the DiSC, you can still share your tendency in the midst of conflict. How does that tendency change based on the context between home, work, and church?

Below are the tendencies of each type:

D – Confrontation

i – Compromise

S – Accommodation

C – Avoidance.

Process   15/30 Minutes

What have you learned about yourself in learning more about healthy conflict? Share with a teammate. What would a loved one say about how you deal with conflict? How self-aware were you of their perspective of how you deal with conflict? What would your next step be in working on how you deal with healthy conflict?

Probe   10/20 Minutes

In thinking about your next steps in dealing with conflict in a healthy manner as a spiritual leader, are your next identified steps goals or Godly work? What shifts would need to be made to make them more Godly work? Share your insights with a teammate.

- How am I different because of prayer and study?

- How am I growing because of my prayer and study encounters?

- How am I maturing as a disciple because of my prayer and study practices?

- How am I inspired to be more because of prayer and study experiences?

Practice   5/10 Minutes

In further development of spiritual habits, it is time to work on stewardship. A tithe is a minimum expectation and not a maximum expectation. Giving is a spiritual practice that one participates in out of the abundance that God provides to each of us. Where are you in moving towards a tithe or beyond? What is the next faithful step in the spiritual practice of the tithe? How are you doing in continuing to keep up with your other spiritual practices from the previous sessions? How are you being held accountable for developing these new spiritual and leadership habits?

If you are not currently generous with your church, you might have some healthy conflict with yourself about how you choose to spend the resources God has entrusted to you.

How will you continue to practice having healthy conflict? If you are married, you might have this conversation with your spouse.

Healthy conflict and healing candor work back and forth in order to process and move through issues.

Potential Resources

Books:

The Anatomy of Peace: Resolving the Heart of Conflict
The Arbinger Institute

Movies:

12 Angry Men
12 O'Clock High

Session Four

Healing Candor

Pray   5/5 Minutes

Prayer for Cleansing and Pardon Psalm 51

(To the leader. A Psalm of David, when the prophet Nathan came to him, after he had gone in to Bathsheba.)

Have mercy on me, O God, according to your steadfast love; according to your abundant mercy blot out my transgressions. Wash me thoroughly from my iniquity, and cleanse me from my sin. For I know my transgressions, and my sin is ever before me. Against you, you alone, have I sinned, and done what is evil in your sight, so that you are justified in your sentence and blameless when you pass judgment. Indeed, I was born guilty, a sinner when my mother conceived me.

You desire truth in the inward being; therefore teach me wisdom in my secret heart. Purge me with hyssop, and I shall be clean; wash me, and I shall be whiter than snow. Let me hear joy and gladness; let the bones that you have crushed rejoice. Hide your face from my sins, and blot out all my iniquities.

Create in me a clean heart, O God, and put a new and right spirit within me. Do not cast me away from your presence, and do not take your holy spirit from me. Restore to me the joy of your salvation, and sustain in me a willing spirit. Then I will teach transgressors your ways, and sinners will return to you. Deliver me from bloodshed, O God, O God of my salvation and my tongue will sing aloud of your deliverance.

O Lord, open my lips, and my mouth will declare your praise. For you have no delight in sacrifice; if I were to give a burnt offering, you would not be pleased. The sacrifice acceptable to God[d] is a broken spirit; a broken and contrite heart, O God, you will not despise. Do good to Zion in your good pleasure; rebuild the walls of Jerusalem, then you will delight in right sacrifices, in burnt offerings and whole burnt offerings; then bulls will be offered on your altar.

For our prayer in this session, use the paper folding evangelistic tool at:

https://gocrossway.org/paper/

Play   20/30 Minutes

Divide the group into two teams. Go to the following website to see the top ten best paper airplane designs. Choose three designs to build for each team (by title and pictures only). Have each team build all three paper airplane designs after watching the how-to video only once. Everyone on the opposing team needs to provide a critique for a better design. Point out a flaw in the building of the plane. After each team has had their work critiqued, each team member needs to share a critique of the critique. For example, how could the critique have been just as effective in communication and outcome with perhaps more grace offered? How was the original critique not clear, or how did it not offer truth telling? After sharing, unpack how this exercise felt for each person. What did you learn about yourself individually? What did you learn about healing candor in this exercise?

Watch KidSpot: "10 of the best paper plane designs."

https://www.kidspot.com.au/things-to-do/outdoor-activities/
outdoor-play/10-of-the-best-paper-plane-designs/news-story/
7f7ac94ddc1c5059f17b25e7c880722e. July 31. 2017.

Ponder   10/15 Minutes

Read I Corinthians 2.
Reflect on verses 10-16. How does this scripture speak to you in terms of healing candor? What can we learn from Paul's teachings?

Read I Corinthians 3.
Reflect on the first four verses. How does this scripture teach us about healing candor? Now reflect on verses 18-23. Again, what insights do you gain about healing candor from this scripture?

Provoke   25/45 Minutes

If you are using the Ted Talk, this exercise will exceed 25 minutes, so plan accordingly.

Engage your team in another round of play this week with the Marshmallow Challenge, an eighteen-minute exercise followed by viewing the accompanying Ted Talk.

Download the instructions here:

https://www.tomwujec.com/marshmallowchallenge

TED Talks:
Wujec, Tom. "Build a tower, build a team." Ted2010.
www.ted.com/talks/tom_wujec_build_a_tower?language=en.
February 2010.

Leading with candor can sometimes be difficult. We often do not speak up when needed because we feel we will not be heard or we will hurt another's feelings. In my experience, I (Kay) find that too often the unsaid moments pass by so quickly and represent so many lost opportunities. How many times have you spoken with someone after a meeting you attended together to learn afterwards both of you had a question or felt something should be said, but neither did? Those are often missed learning opportunities for everyone.

Most often when you are thinking something, others in the conversation are thinking it, too. We often get stuck in wanting to stay safe. We don't practice candor because we believe we need to hold our relationships with one another in higher regard than the overall good of the group, organization, or mission.

For example, I (Kay) often see church boards or leadership teams not speak truthfully, resulting in teams being stuck or even ineffective. They don't speak up because they value relationships with one another more than they value the mission of the church to make disciples. It seems we would rather maintain our relationships with one another than see others know Jesus Christ.

Recall a time when you have been in a situation where candor was not practiced. What was the outcome? What could have been the outcome? What was the gap?

How might we design better churches and ways to reach new people by being open to Healing Candor in the design process. What might your church need to try?

Process   10/30 Minutes

Consider your spiritual leadership skills in healing candor. How would you rate your development level? Share your evaluation with a teammate. What would a faithful step in development be for you? The second step? Who will hold you accountable for these steps? What are you learning about yourself as a spiritual leadership in this process? What has surprised you? What has been confirmed in what you already knew about yourself as a leader?

Practice   10/20 Minutes

To further develop our habits as a spiritual leader, it is now time to consider how we serve. Serving can take on a variety of roles. One can serve on a ministry team inside the church. One can serve in ministry that reaches outside the lives of those who are already a part of the congregation. Often, we stretch ourselves most as spiritual leaders when we are working in ministry areas that are more outwardly focused and working in the mission of reaching new people. Sometimes working inside the church is not always stretching our spiritual and leadership habits.

Where are you currently serving inside and outside the church? Are you serving in places which match your spiritual and leadership gifts? Would you want to make any shifts in the places you are serving? If so, what and when? Share with your teammate.

For even the Son of Man did not come to be served, but to serve, and to give his life as a ransom for many.

Mark 10:45 (NIV)

How are you doing with the spiritual habits you have worked on in previous sessions (i.e. praying, studying, giving)? What is going well? Where are the gaps? How will you fill those gaps? Share your insights and next faithful steps with your teammate.

Probe   5/20 Minutes

Review your next faithful steps from above. Are you stretching yourself as a spiritual leader or are you playing it safe? Are you stretching yourself? How are you holding back? What is keeping you from being all in? Where is God stretching you these days? How are you allowing God to stretch you? Process these questions and share with your teammate.

[1-4]After this, Jesus went across the Sea of Galilee (some call it Tiberias). A huge crowd followed him, attracted by the miracles they had seen him do among the sick. When he got to the other side, he climbed a hill and sat down, surrounded by his disciples. It was nearly time for the Feast of Passover, kept annually by the Jews.

[5-6]When Jesus looked out and saw that a large crowd had arrived, he said to Philip, "Where can we buy bread to feed these people?" He said this to stretch Philip's faith. He already knew what he was going to do.

John 6:1-6 The Message (MSG)

Where might you need to follow up with someone with whom you have had conflict with a time of healing candor? If the person is alive, reach out to them. Go see them as soon as possible. If they are no longer with us, write a letter, expressing what you would have said.

• How am I different because of my witness?

• How am I growing because of my witness encounters?

• How am I maturing as a disciple because of my witness practices?

• How am I inspired to be more because of my witness experiences?

Potential Resources

Books:

Managing Transitions by William Bridges

Crucial Conversations by Kerry Patterson

Movies:

Sister Act

Session Five

Humbled Confidence

Pray

Let us then approach God's throne of grace with confidence, so that we may receive mercy and find grace to help us in our time of need.

Hebrews 4:16 (NRSV)

Dear God,

You know my heart and you know that I love you. I'm trying to do my best to follow after you, but sometimes I get tripped up. Sometimes I lose focus. Sometimes I forget who I am in you and start looking to the world to tell me who I am. On the days when my confidence is fading fast, build me up again. Remind me of the simple truth that confidence can only be found in chasing after you. I can walk around confident knowing I am loved. I can walk around confident knowing I am enough. I can live knowing I have been rescued, free and called to do great things. Help me remember these things, wonderful Father.

In Jesus' Name, Amen.[25]

---

25 Gaskill, Laura. "A Prayer for Confidence." https://www.ibelieve.com/faith/a-prayer-for-confidence.html. May 24, 2016.

Play   5/5 Minutes

Sometimes gaining confidence comes with working with others within a team. Gather in groups of two or three people. Each team is provided two pieces of similar paper. The team first plans their paper airplane design. Then, the team is challenged to build a rough model using the first piece of paper. Finally, each team uses the second piece of paper to build their final paper airplane prototype. Each team then competes for furthest distance, highest altitude, and best speed.

After the competition is complete, discuss how confidence was built through teaming. How did teaming improve distance, altitude, and speed? How did using time to plan build confidence in the design and performance? How did the planning and prototype improve distance, altitude, and speed?

Ponder   20/30 Minutes

Read 1 Corinthians, Chapters 8 and 9 (MSG)

Re-read 1 Corinthians 8:1-3

In this scripture there is a reference that our humbled hearts can help us more than our proud minds. Spend some time in your group discussing this passage and its meaning as it pertains to the humbled confidence leadership trait.

Re-read 1 Corinthians 8:7

This passage refers to how know-it-alls can begin to treat others as know-nothings. It goes on to further speak about this type of know-it-all as insensitive. Discuss your thoughts and feelings about know-it-alls and making others feel like know-nothings.

Re-read 1 Corinthians 8:10-13

These verses refer to one's pathway of faith development. We all recognize people are in different places in their faith journey. Discuss with your partner or group how humbled confidence plays into the sensitivity of walking alongside people who may be in a different place in their spiritual journey.

Re-read 1 Corinthians 9

Reflect on how Paul was instructing the Corinthian church in humbled confidence. Cite specific scripture that point to this valuable leadership lesson. Reflect on how this passage affects your feelings on humbled confidence as it relates to leadership.

Provoke   25/45 Minutes

Watch this Ted Talk together:
Red Zone Chickens: Tamm, Jim. *"Cultivating Collaboration: Don't Be So Defensive!"* TEDx Talks.
https://www.youtube.com/watch?v=vjSTNv4gyMM. May 26, 2015.

How can dealing with your own defensiveness show a humbled confidence? Where have you been in the Red Zone in recent days? What experiences and habits help you stay in the Green Zone?

Orville and Wilbur Wright were the ultimate example of humbled confidence. These brothers could have easily given up on any one of their failed flights. Yet, they knew flight was the future. They failed boldly. They were humbled to realize that failures led to ultimate success. They were confident enough to keep going, but humbled enough to learn from their failed experiments.

Reflect on a time where overconfidence kept you moving forward even in light of potential or actual failure. What did you learn about yourself in this experience? Did humility play into the situation? If so, how? If not, explain. Share your reflections with your partner or group.

Process   15/30 Minutes

For you to further develop in the leadership trait of humbled confidence, what faithful step will you be willing to make? Second step? Who will hold you accountable for the accomplishment of these steps? When will these steps be completed? Humbled confidence is often the result of failure or falling short. When we fall short, we are called to confess and then repent in order to be reconciled. Where might you need to confess and repent in order to grow into humbled confidence?

Probe   10/20 Minutes

Reflect on your action steps above. Are these personal goals or your Godly work? Make any shifts necessary to make sure you are developing as a spiritual leader, not only a leader.

- How am I different because of my giving and generosity?

- How am I growing because of my giving and generosity?

- How am I maturing as a disciple because of my giving and generosity?

- How am I inspired to be more because of my giving and generosity?

Practice

As you begin to practice humbled confidence more fully, your next step in being a spiritual leader is to ensure you are building spiritual friendships. Who are you being mentored by who is a more mature disciple and can hold you accountable for your spiritual walk, specifically leading with humbled confidence? Check in with a mentor to discuss your next steps and how you are progressing in your humbled confidence.

As you develop as a spiritual leader, who are you spending time with in your spiritual circle of friends? Who else is on this same type of leadership development journey that you can help along their pathway? Who might you befriend this week? Who is your accountability partner?

As you live out your membership vows, you have promised to serve. Your spiritual practice to accompany your humbled confidence leadership is the spiritual practice of serving. How would you rate yourself on serving? Your church? Your community? The world? What improvements would you like to make in this spiritual practice? How will you serve in this coming week? Month? Year?

Potential Resources

Books:

Hero Maker by Ferguson and Bird

Movies:

Black Panther

Story:

Brown, Cody. "The Difference Between Confidence and Arrogance is Empathy."

https://medium.com/@CodyBrown/the-difference-between-confi-dence-and-arrogance-is-empathy-91aaf9cb949b. December 12, 2013.

Podcasts:

The Dance of Humility and Confidence. Howes, Lewis. "There's a Bigger Story."

https://lewishowes.com/podcast/the-battle-between-confi-dence-and-humility/. Accessed May 15, 2019.

TED Talks:

The Power of Vulnerability by Brené Brown. "The Power of Vulnerability."

https://www.youtube.com/watch?v=iCvmsMzlF7o. January 3, 2011.

Session Six

Hope-filled Collaborations

Pray   5/5 Minutes

Today we will start our time together with a collaborative prayer. One person starts the prayer. Each person will add a sentence or two to the prayer. You can choose who will end the prayer and/or you can choose to close the prayer jointly reciting the Lord's Prayer together.

Play   20/30 Minutes

In this session one paper airplane will be built by the entire team. Take time communicating and planning the build. What is the intended outcome of the design? Sleekest design? Stay in flight a certain distance? Most airtime? Something else? You only get one chance and one piece of paper. Every person on the team must share in the building experience. It is to be a collaborative experience. Once the airplane is built, evaluate the outcome against expectations.

How did the collaboration go? What did you learn about one another in the process?

Ponder 10/15 Minutes

Read Exodus 17
Describe how Joshua, Aaron, and Hur were part of hope-filled collaboration with Moses. What would have happened with this spirit of collaboration? Discuss the symbolism of holding up the hands of Moses. Who holds up your hands? Whose hands are you holding up?

Read 1 Corinthians 11:33
At the Lord's table we are to be reverent and courteous to one another. How does this scripture reflect on how we are to treat one another in hope-filled collaboration?

Spend some time thinking and sharing how these two scriptures collectively speak to the spirit of hope-filled collaboration.

Provoke 25/45 Minutes

Fun little teamwork video:
ChoozaBooza. "Funny Animation: How Animals Work In Team." YouTube.com.
https://www.youtube.com/watch?v=kWhZRahpgXE.
Accessed June 2, 2019.

Video:
Edmundson, Amy. "How to turn a group of strangers into a team." TED Salon: Brightline Initiative.
https://www.ted.com/talks/amy_edmondson_how_to_turn_a_group_of_strangers_into_a_team?language=en.
October 2017.

The Wright brothers were a team. It was within their collaborations together that they learned from one another and gained confidence to keep trying. They also collaborated with others. They used their experience in building bikes to aid them in building airplanes. They learned from other aviators' experiments and failed attempts. They never gave up. They continued to be hope-filled. Reflect on a time when you were tempted to give up, but because of others around you, you persevered. How did having collaborators around you offering hope change the outcome of the situation? What did you learn about yourself and your leadership in this experience?

Process   10/30 Minutes

Reflect on what you have discovered as a hope-filled collaborator. How would you rate yourself as a hope-filled collaborator? What first step would you want to take to become a better hope-filled collaborative leader? Second step? What potential obstacles would need to be overcome to take these next faithful steps? Who will hold you accountable for these steps? When will you complete these steps? What resourcing might you need to make these steps?

Probe   10/20 Minutes

Take a look at your identified next steps. Are these personal goals? Or is it the Godly work you are called to do?

What modifications, if any, might you need to make to ensure this is your next faithful step in developing as a hope-filled collaborative leader?

145

- How am I different because of service?

- How am I growing because of my service?

- How am I maturing as a disciple because of my service?

- How am I inspired to be more because of service experiences?

Practice

Coaching has not just become a nice "add-on" tool for every ministry leader. Instead coaching has developed into a "must-have" for ministry leaders. Rev. Val Hastings, the founder of Coaching4Clergy cast this vision quite some time ago: "a global vision of Every Pastor, Ministry Staff and Church Leader a Coach." In his experience as a United Methodist pastor, he found coaching to be the catalyst in becoming the most effective leader in his local church. As a credentialed coach myself, I (Kay) found that gaining coaching skills allowed me to develop more fully as a leader than any other type of experience or training I have ever had the privilege of participating in. It is in this spirit that we will be launching leaders with coaching. In the wrap-up stage in the final section of this book, you will be working with a coach while also becoming a coach for the next generation of leaders.

Coaching is a mixture of showing up with an increased level of curiosity with another person without judgment or preconceived ideas. In the experience, the coach is helping the coachee clarify the current reality of a situation the coachee wants to work on along with the desired outcome.

Through powerful questions, the coach helps the coachee close the gap between current and future. The result is a future-moving motion of action steps towards the desirable outcome. The coach comes alongside the coachee for self-reflection, accountability, building awareness, encouragement, and support. Again, coaching is a hope-filled collaborative leadership approach rather than a top-down leadership approach. Most people are much more open to being coached than being told what to do. Therefore, we highly recommend coaching to develop the leadership trait of hope-filled collaboration. Collaboration and coaching are both a spiritual practice and habit of effective leadership.

Potential Resources

Book:
Emotionally Healthy Spirituality by Peter Scazzero
1-2-3 Coach by J. Val Hastings. Find it at
https://coaching4clergy.com/free-resources/.

Movies:
The Blindside
A Bug's Life

TED Talks:
www.ted.com/topics/collaboration. Many videos are available here.

Wrap Up

In the scripture below, notice how all six leadership habits appear in Moses' leadership. What a great role model Moses was and is.

The Charge and The Launch

Moses went on and addressed these words to all Israel. He said, "I'm 120 years old today. I can't get about as I used to. And God told me, 'You're not going to cross this Jordan River.'

"God, your God, will cross the river ahead of you and destroy the nations in your path so that you may dispossess them. (And Joshua will cross the river before you, as God said he would.) God will give the nations the same treatment he gave the kings of the Amorites, Sihon and Og, and their land; he'll destroy them. God will hand the nations over to you, and you'll treat them exactly as I have commanded you.

"Be strong. Take courage. Don't be intimidated. Don't give them a second thought because God, your God, is striding ahead of you. He's right there with you. He won't let you down; he won't leave you."
(Humbled Confidence)

Then Moses summoned Joshua. He said to him with

*all Israel watching, "Be strong. Take courage. You
will enter the land with this people, this land that
God promised their ancestors that he'd give them.
You will make them the proud possessors of it. God
is striding ahead of you. He's right there with you.
He won't let you down; he won't leave you. Don't be
intimidated. Don't worry."*

*Moses wrote out this Revelation and gave it to the
priests, the sons of Levi, who carried the Chest of
the Covenant of God, and to all the leaders of Israel.
And he gave these orders: "At the end of every seven
years, the Year-All-Debts-Are-Canceled, during the
pilgrim Festival of Booths when everyone in Israel
comes to appear in the Presence of God, your God, at
the place he designates, read out this Revelation to
all Israel, with everyone listening. Gather the people
together—men, women, children, and the foreign-
ers living among you—so they can listen well, so
they may learn to live in holy awe before God, your
God, and diligently keep everything in this Revelation. And do this so that their children, who don't
yet know all this, will also listen and learn to live
in holy awe before God, your God, for as long as
you live on the land that you are crossing over the
Jordan to possess."* (Helpful Conversation)

*God spoke to Moses: "You are about to die. So call
Joshua. Meet me in the Tent of Meeting so that I can
commission him."*

*So Moses and Joshua went and stationed themselves
in the Tent of Meeting. God appeared in the Tent in a
Pillar of Cloud. The Cloud was near the entrance of
the Tent of Meeting.* (Hope-filled Collaboration)

*God spoke to Moses: "You're about to die and be
buried with your ancestors. You'll no sooner be in
the grave than this people will be up and whoring
after the foreign gods of this country that they are
entering. They will abandon me and violate my
Covenant that I've made with them. I'll get angry,
oh so angry! I'll walk off and leave them on their*

own, won't so much as look back at them. Then many calamities and disasters will devastate them because they are defenseless. They'll say, 'Isn't it because our God wasn't here that all this evil has come upon us?' But I'll stay out of their lives, keep looking the other way because of all their evil: they took up with other gods!"

"But for right now, copy down this song and teach the People of Israel to sing it by heart. They'll have it then as my witness against them. When I bring them into the land that I promised to their ancestors, a land flowing with milk and honey, and they eat and become full and get fat and then begin fooling around with other gods and worshiping them, and then things start falling apart, many terrible things happening, this song will be there with them as a witness to who they are and what went wrong. Their children won't forget this song; they'll be singing it. Don't think I don't know what they are already scheming to do, and they're not even in the land yet, this land I promised them." (Healing Candor)

So Moses wrote down this song that very day and taught it to the People of Israel. Then God commanded Joshua son of Nun saying, "Be strong. Take courage. You will lead the People of Israel into the land I promised to give them. And I'll be right there with you."

After Moses had finished writing down the words of this Revelation in a book, right down to the last word, he ordered the Levites who were responsible for carrying the Chest of the Covenant of God, saying, "Take this Book of Revelation and place it alongside the Chest of the Covenant of God, your God. Keep it there as a witness."

"I know what rebels you are, how stubborn and willful you can be. Even today, while I'm still alive and present with you, you're rebellious against God. How much worse when I've died! So gather the leaders of the tribes and the officials here. I

have something I need to say directly to them with Heaven and Earth as witnesses. I know that after I die you're going to make a mess of things, abandoning the way I commanded, inviting all kinds of evil consequences in the days ahead. You're determined to do evil in defiance of God—I know you are—deliberately provoking his anger by what you do." (Healthy Conflict)

So with everyone in Israel gathered and listening, Moses taught them the words of this song, from start to finish.

Deuteronomy 31 (MSG)

Holistic Coaching

The participants in launching leaders have now completed ground school. They are now ready to take flight. But remember, before a pilot flies solo, the pilot must spend time with a flight instructor. The flight instructor determines when the pilot is ready to fly solo. Even after flying solo, pilots must log a certain number of flying hours, take-offs, and landings before they are ready to be tested to obtain their pilot's license. Only then are they able to have passengers in the plane with them.

Just like our pilots, our leaders still need some resourcing and equipping even though they have graduated from ground school. Once a prospective pilot graduates from ground school, she/he is now ready for a flight instructor. We recommend pairing each of your newly graduated ground school participants with a flight instructor or what you might refer to as a leadership coach. This coach may be someone within the congregation or may even be someone outside. We recommend the coach be someone who is very familiar with the process, has graduated from the process, and/or has become a mature spiritual leader. It would also be helpful for the coach to have some coach training (see Coaching4Clergy.com). The coach's role is to continue to help guide and resource the leader being both an encourager and one who holds him/her accountable to the process and the expected development. Coaching also supports each new leader in their perseverance and pursuant of gaining more and more skills as a leader to stay the course.

Don't overlook this critical part of the process. Without ongoing coaching, the new leader may find themselves not upholding their new habits and/or not continuing to live into their best possible leadership capabilities. The flight instructor or coach will help the newly launched leader identify progress, gaps, and faithful next steps. We suggest a minimal once a month check-in with the coach. The person or team responsible for the leadership development process should have a tracking system in place to ensure this part of the process continues. She/he holds both the coach and the participants accountable for this important step in launching leaders. This is a minimum of a six-month coaching relationship, but may need to go as long as a year. Some people derive the much needed and appreciated support, encouragement, and accountability for coaching that it becomes a lifelong leadership development tool. Once a person has completed ground school and has gone through the flight instructor or coaching phase, they may likely be one of the next round of coaches or flight instructors for the next class of participants in the launching leader intentional leadership development process.

As part of the church's on-going launching leaders commitment, the church may want to create and maintain a leadership development progress chart (tracking or similar). This may include the number of ground school participants, the number in holistic coaching with their flight instructor, and those leaders who are now flying solo. A church might also want to track how many launching leaders participants have completed all the steps and are now a coach/flight instructor for new participants. Many would say that the number of leaders we are raising up and sending out is a much more important statistic to track that many of the other vital signs for measuring church vitality. Multiplication of leaders brings multiplication of other signs of church vitality such as worship attendance, professions of faith, baptisms, etc.

Not an Expert and Never Finished

While some people are continuously developing and learning, it is really difficult to refer to anyone as an expert these days. When we find a so-called expert, we rely on that person wholly for answers and expertise. Often times, experts are self-identified and not necessarily experts identified by those on the outside. We might also suggest that in our fast-paced society, things are changing at such rapid rates that it is just too difficult for any one person to keep up with everything. While some certainly have more experience than others in given fields, beware of anyone who claims to be an expert.

This also speaks into this leadership development process. Just like disciples are never fully formed and mature, leaders are never fully formed and mature. We are all always in continuous formation and evolution to become the best versions of ourselves to most fully do the work God created us to do. We must never come to the conclusion that we are fully developed leaders. We must make ourselves open to continuous learning and growing. For when we believe we are finished, we are indeed finished. Some of the wisest people who have ever lived were still learning until their last breath was taken.

Commitment

Leadership development takes commitment. It takes commitment from someone in the church to make it a priority such as the pastor, nominations committee, and/or lay leader. It takes commitment for someone to lead a group (and continue to lead groups) through the development process. It takes commitment from the participants to stick with the process. It takes commitment to go through the coaching portion of the process to gain momentum and ongoing healthy spiritual and leadership habits. It takes commitment on the part of the coach to hold the new leader accountable to the process. It takes commitment to start the second class once the first class has completed ground school. But please allow us to offer this as you begin to hear the size of the commitment this will take: **it will be so worth it.** As we stated in the foreword, most churches are crying out for leadership. Most churches have no leadership development process. When leaders are launched and those new leaders launch more leaders, the church can once again have leaders not only in the church, but in society. Imagine how the world could change if the church were to once again launch spiritual leaders!

Sometimes people have never been given the opportunity to lead. They may very well have the ability to be a leader, but were just never given the chance. Just like the three characters who traveled along with Dorothy to see the Wizard, the leaders already have what they are searching or long for. They just didn't realize it. The lion wanted courage. The tin man wanted a heart. And the scarecrow wanted a brain. All those things were already present. They just did not yet know. This process helps uncover the leadership qualities that are hiding inside. Help people discover their own God-given gifts!

Wrap Up

As the first class begins to wrap up their time together, we suggest having a time together with the group one final time before they set off to begin flying as leaders. Bring together the class, the leader of the class, and the coaches each participant will be working with over the coming months. This is a great time of celebration, commitment to the next steps, and "loving thy neighbor as thyself."

Use this time for each participant to share what the experience has meant for them, what they have learned overall, the most meaningful portion of the time together, what's next for them in the leadership development process, introduce their coaches, etc. This might also be a time to share a foot washing experience as a sign of the servant leader's heart. This might be a time of breaking bread with one another as a sign of celebration and covenant. This group may even want to come together for reunion gatherings from time to time to check in with one another and hear about next steps in their own leadership development and celebrate those steps with one another.

Once leaders have graduated both ground school and flight training with their flight instructor/holistic coach, your congregation might like to offer a ceremony where launched leaders earn "their wings."

156

This should be a great time of celebration for both the leader and the congregation.

What's Next

Where is God taking me next? We never know what God has in store for us. But when we have equipped ourselves to be spiritual leaders, we are surely more ready for the faithful steps God has in store for us. Remember, at any given time there are three intersecting circles: God, Me, and Context. When we are a launched leader, we can be more fully aware of all three and be best prepared for what's next.

God bless you on your flight!

Launch these leaders and begin the next class of launching leaders!

Potential Resources

Books:
Emotionally Healthy Leader by Peter Scazzero

Movies:
Remember the Titans

Also from Kay Kotan

IMPACT!
*Reclaiming the Call
of Lay Ministry*
Kay Kotan & Blake Bradford

Other Books

from Market Square

marketsquarebooks.com

Wesleyan Grace Theology

Dr. Donald Haynes

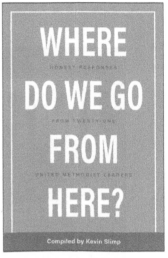

Where Do We Go From Here?

20 United Methodist Writers

The Good Folks of Lennox Valley

Kevin Slimp

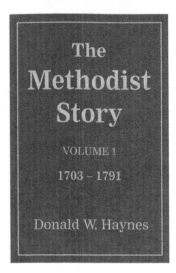

The Methodist Story
Volume I • 1703-1791

Dr. Donald Haynes

Grow Your Faith

with these books from Market Square

marketsquarebooks.com

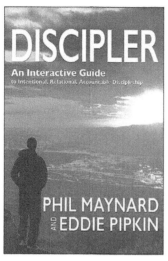

Discipler

Phil Maynard & Eddie Pipkin

Hear It, See It, Risk It

Steve Cordle

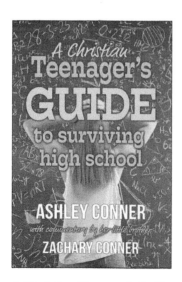

**A Christian Teenager's Guide
to Surviving High School**

Ashley Conner

Understanding Your Call

*11 Biblical Figures Understand
Their Calls from God*

by 10 United Methodist Leaders

Grow Your Faith

with these books from Market Square

marketsquarebooks.com

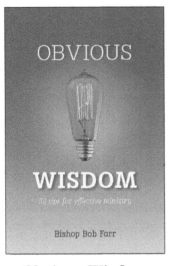

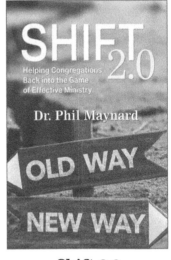

Obvious Wisdom

Bishop Bob Farr

Shift 2.0

Phil Maynard

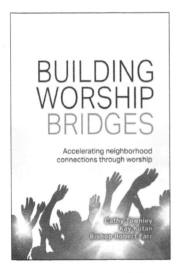

Building Worship Bridges

Cathy Townley

Get Out of that Box!

Anne Bosarge

Latest Titles
from Market Square Books
marketsquarebooks.com

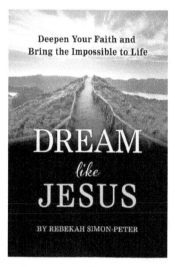

Dream Like Jesus
Bring the Impossible to Life

Rebekah Simon-Peter

From Franchise
To Local Dive

Available November 2019

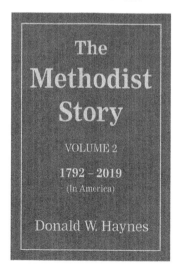

The Methodist Story
Volume 2 • 1792-2019

Dr. Donald W. Haynes

From Heaven
To Earth
Christmas for New Believers, Old Believers and Nonbelievers

Now Available
by Kay Kotan & Blake Bradford

Revised and Expanded Second Edition